D0658656

The Chartered
Institute of Marketing

CIM Companion:

customer communications

CIM Publishing

CIM Publishing

The Chartered Institute of Marketing
Moor Hall
Cookham
Berkshire
SL6 9QH

www.cim.co.uk

First published 2002

Series Editors: Mark Stuart and John Ling.

The publishers believe that the contents of this book contribute to debate and offer practical advice. No responsibility will be taken by the publishers for any damage or loss arising from following or interpreting the advice given in this publication. No sexism is implied by the use of the pronoun 'he' or 'his', which is used to avoid ungrammatical or clumsy language.

It is the publisher's policy to use paper manufactured from sustainable forests.

British Library Cataloguing in Publication Data
A CIP catalogue record for this book can be obtained from the British Library.

ISBN 0 902130 97 8

Printed and bound by The Cromwell Press, Trowbridge, Wiltshire.
Cover design by Marie-Claire Bonhommet.

contents

Study guide

This Companion is written to complement the recommended core text, *Communicating with Customers* by Patrick Forsyth and published by Orion Business. It aims to offer you support either as an individual or group learner as you move along the road to becoming a competent and proficient marketer. This is a process of learning that has two important elements:

Understanding marketing concepts and their application

The study text in the following Sessions has been deliberately written to highlight the concepts that you will need to grasp as you start to understand marketing fundamentals, what marketing can achieve, and how it is implemented. The material is described briefly and concisely, to enable you to cover a range of key material at first stage level. It does not attempt to be fully comprehensive, and you should read widely from other sources, including the recommended course text (readings are specified for relevant Sessions from this book and two others, and shown in Table 3 which follows), the marketing press and national newspapers, to develop your understanding of the concepts introduced here. More comprehensive marketing textbooks are detailed on the module reading list; these provide a wider context for the concepts explained in this Companion, and provide more Case Studies and examples to illustrate marketing in practice.

Developing the skills to implement marketing activity

Equally important in the journey towards marketing excellence is the acquisition, development and refining of a range of skills that are required on a daily basis by marketers across all industries and sectors. These transferable skills hold the key to the effective implementation of the marketing techniques explored in the study text. The focus of the practical activities in this book is on seven key skills for marketers:

- Using ICT and the Internet.
- Using financial information and metrics.
- Presenting information.
- Working with others.
- Applying business law.
- Improving and developing own learning.
- Problem solving.

The first five of these key skills are linked to the activities shown in Table 1 that follows.

Improving and developing own learning is achieved by undertaking the Projects that are at the end of each Session.

Problem solving is achieved through the Case Study and questions at the end of each Session.

Using the Companion

The syllabus for the module has been broken down into twelve Sessions, each of which covers approximately the same proportion of the content. Every student brings with them to their studies different levels of experience, as a customer, from previous studies, and possibly from working in marketing or sales. You should therefore be aware that, whilst you may need to spend considerable time on an unfamiliar area of the syllabus, you may make up this time when studying another area with which you are more familiar.

Each Session has a number of short Activities, which you should try to complete as you work your way through the text. These will help you to check your understanding of the material, and brief feedback is provided at the end of each Session, so that you can compare your answers. Each Session has three activities except Session 1 which has four activities.

At the end of each Session there is also a Case Study and a series of related questions, which may be problem solving questions or designed to help check your understanding of some of the main issues. Many of the Case Studies have been taken from past examination papers, so you can use them to help prepare you for this type of activity within your exam. Try to complete these without reference to your notes, or the Session text, and then compare your answers with some key points that are given at the end of the Companion, in Appendix 1.

Finally, you will see that there is a past examination paper in Appendix 3. This can help you with your revision, examination technique, and preparation. Allow time nearer to your actual examination to complete the paper under examination conditions – that is, allow three hours of uninterrupted time, and complete the paper without reference to your notes or the study material. When you have completed the exercise, you can compare your answers to the notes in Appendix 4. If either your approach to the exercise, or the comparison of your answers highlight areas of particular weakness, you should refer back to the text and re-read the relevant Session, together with the chapters of the supporting textbook.

The main approach taken in this Companion is a practical one of 'hands on'. The text concentrates on what marketers in organisations do in a tactical role. Additional projects are suggested that involve some further research. No feedback is provided for these but you may wish to compare answers with other marketers studying at the same level.

The five knowledge and skills elements of the syllabus are covered in a different order to the syllabus (reproduced in Appendix 2) due to the integrative nature of the individual constituents.

The following table identifies how the knowledge and skill requirements of the syllabus are covered in the Companion.

Syllabus Knowledge and Skill Requirements	Companion Session
1.1 Explain what is meant by the terms 'customer', 'stakeholder' and 'user'.	Session 1
1.2 Demonstrate the fundamental importance of 'customers' to all forms of organisations, including services and the need to clearly identify them.	Session 1
1.3 Describe the link between the marketing concept, a customer focus and relationship marketing.	Session 1
1.4 Appreciate the need for effective internal and external customer communications and their link to and role in maintaining customer focus, developing and sustaining good customer relations and relationship marketing in creating loyalty and customer retention.	Sessions 1 and 2
1.5 List the factors that cause change in customers and the subsequent impact on marketing programmes.	Session 5

2.1 Explain the difference between consumer buyer behaviour and organisational buyer behaviour.	Session 6
2.2 Explain the importance of understanding buyer behaviour.	Session 6
2.3 Describe the Decision Making Unit (DMU) and the roles of its constituents.	Session 6
2.4 The Decision Making Process (DMP) for consumers and organisations.	Session 6
2.5 The impact and effect of the DMU and the DMP on the communications mix.	Session 6
3.1 Explain the concept of, and need for, an integrated marketing communications approach and the links between communications and marketing planning.	Session 7
3.2 Explain the role and importance of promotion in marketing.	Session 7
3.3 Explain the structure and function of the communication process.	Session 3
3.4 Describe the tools of promotion (the promotion mix).	Session 7
3.5 Explain the planning process for developing and implementing promotional strategies and individual elements of the promotional mix.	Sessions 7, 8 and 9
3.6 Explain how above-the-line and below-the-line activities are used.	Sessions 7 and 9
3.7 Explain the key stages and considerations when developing and designing advertisements.	Session 9

3.8 Describe the role and scope of PR and its contribution to the promotional mix.	Session 8
3.9 Explain the role of corporate identity, brand image and logos in corporate communication with customers.	Session 11
3.10 Distinguish between the different forms of integrated mail media, such as direct mail leaflets and mail order advertising.	Session 9
3.11 Explain the role of Point of Sale (POS) material and how it is developing in response to changing customer needs.	Session 10
3.12 Explain the role of packaging in the promotions mix.	Session 11
3.13 Describe the role of exhibitions as a communications tool and their role in promotions.	Session 10
3.14 Explain the role of Information and Communications Technology (ICT) in communications, including digital TV and interactive marketing.	Session 12
3.15 Describe current trends and developments in promotions and their impact on organisations.	Sessions 7 and 12
4.1 Describe the communication process and explain the importance and the advantages and disadvantages of different types of communication in a variety of face to face situations.	Session 3
4.2 Identify barriers to communication and explain how they can be avoided and overcome.	Session 3

4.3 Explain the communications planning process to produce effective strategies for improving alternative communications formats.	Sessions 3 and 4
4.4 Explain the importance of effective body language, tone, verbal and listening skills in communication and strategies for developing and improving verbal, non-verbal and listening skills.	Session 3
4.5 Interpret, summarise and present oral, written and graphical information.	Session 3
4.6 Explain key communication factors to consider in meetings, including arranging and convening a meeting, documentation involved and strategies for conducting a meeting.	Session 4
4.7 Plan, prepare and deliver a presentation using appropriate and effective visual aids and media.	Session 4
4.8 Use a variety of formats to communicate with internal and external customers including telephone, letters, memoranda, notices, reports and emails.	Session 3
5.1 Explain the concept of customer care and its importance in consumer, business to business, not-for-profit and public sector organisations.	Session 5
5.2 Explain the importance of quality and customer care and methods of achieving quality.	Session 5
5.3 Explain the relationship between customer care, customer focus and relationship marketing.	Session 1

5.4 Explain the importance of obtaining customer feedback and devising contingencies for dealing with customer complaints.	Session 5
5.5 Describe how to plan and establish a customer care programme.	Session 5
5.6 Demonstrate an understanding of how ICT is used in customer service, for example through the use of databases.	Session 2

Table 1 – Key skills

The activities are related to the key skills as shown in the following table:

	Using ICT and Internet	Using financial information and metrics	Presenting information	Working with others	Applying business law	Improving and developing own learning	Problem solving
Session 1	1.3	–	1.2 1.4	1.1	–	Project activities	Case Study
Session 2	2.2	2.3	–	2.1	–	Project activities	Case Study
Session 3	3.2	–	3.1, 3.3	–	–	Project activities	Case Study
Session 4	4.3	–	4.1	4.2	–	Project activities	Case Study
Session 5	–	–	5.1 5.1	5.2	–	Project activities	Case Study
Session 6	–	–	6.2 6.3	6.1	–	Project activities	Case Study
Session 7	7.3	–	–	7.1	7.2	Project activities	Case Study
Session 8	–	–	8.2	8.1, 8.3	–	Project activities	Case Study
Session 9	–	–	–	9.1 9.2	9.3	Project activities	Case Study
Session 10	–	–	10.2	10.1 10.3	–	Project activities	Case Study
Session 11	11.2	–	–	11.1 11.3	–	Project activities	Case Study
Session 12	12.2, 12.3	–	12.1	–	–	Project activities	Case Study

Table 2 – Web sites

This is a standard list of web sites produced for the Certificate level Companions.

CIM	
www.cim.co.uk	
www.connectedinmarketing.com/cim/ index.cfm	
www.cimvirtualinstitute.com	
www.marketingportal.cim.co.uk	Includes CIM Marketing Trends Surveys (MTS).
Advertising	
www.adslogans.co.uk	Online database of advertising slogans enabling marketers to check whether a slogan is already in use.
www.nielson-netratings.com	Details on current banner advertising.
www.ipa.co.uk	Institute of Practitioners in Advertising.
www.asa.org.uk	Advertising Standards Agency.
Direct Marketing	
www.dma.org.uk	Direct Marketing Association.
www.theidm.co.uk	Institute of Direct Marketing.
E-commerce	
www.shopping.yahoo.com	Browse retail sites.
www.ecommercetimes.com	Daily e-news.
www.amazon.co.uk	Customer focused operation.
Events	
www.e-bulletin.com	Guide to exhibitions, events and resources.
www.venuefinder.com	International venue and event suppliers directory.
General Marketing	
www.new-marketing.org	Research updates into new marketing issues, customer segmentation and repercussions for marketing practitioners.

Legislation/Codes of Conduct	
www.wapforum.org	Industry Association responsible for creating the standards for WAP (Wireless Application Protocol).
Public Relations	
www.prnewswire.co.uk	UK media monitoring service – reviews mentions in all media types (print, online publications and broadcast).
www.prsource.co.uk	PR and marketing information sources.
Secondary data sources	
www.keynote.co.uk	Market research reports.
www.verdict.co.uk	Retail research reports.
www.datamonitor.com	Market analysis providing global data collection and in-depth analysis across any industry.
www.store.eiu.com	Economist Intelligence Unit providing country-specific global business analysis.
www.mintel.com	Consumer market research.
www.royalmail.co.uk	General marketing advice and information.
www.ft.com	Financial Times online newspaper and archives.
www.afxpress.com	Business news plus industry trends.
www.caci.co.uk	ACORN classification of residential neighbourhoods.
www.isi.gov.uk	Information Society site with details of government projects, pending legislation etc.
www.worldmarketing.org	World Marketing Association.

Table 3 – Background reading

The following references are suggested background readings for each Session. It is suggested that the student undertake this reading before studying the relevant Companion Session. Reading from additional texts is also required. Please see relevant syllabus on CIM web site.

Session	Reading from Core Text: ***Communicating with Customers*** by Patrick Forsyth, published by Orion Business. Reading from Additional Text: ***Effective Communication*** by Richard Blundell, published by Prentice-Hall. Reading from Additional Text: ***Cybermarketing*** by Bickerton, Bickerton and Pardesi, published by Butterworth-Heinemann.
Session 1	**Communicating with Customers:** Chapter 1 – The opportunity. **Effective Communication:** Chapter 6 – The organisational dimension. **Cybermarketing:** Chapter 1 – Marketing with the Internet.
Session 2	**Communicating with Customers:** Chapter 10 – Internal customers.
Session 3	**Communicating with Customers:** Chapter 3 – Communication: the fundamental principles, Chapter 6 – Communications: putting it in writing, Chapter 7 – Communications: face-to-face, Chapter 12 – A co-ordinated approach. **Effective Communication:** Chapter 2 – Barriers to communication, Chapter 3 – Words: using language, Chapter 4 – Pictures: using images, Chapter 8 – Business letters and direct mail, Chapter 9 – Reports, memos and briefings, Chapter 13 – Interviews and listening skills.
Session 4	**Effective Communication:** Chapter 10 – Making presentations, Chapter 11 – Meetings, teams and negotiations.
Session 5	**Communicating with Customers:** Chapter 8 – Handling complaints, Chapter 9 – Difficult people, Chapter 11 – Systems and procedures.
Session 6	**Communicating with Customers:** Chapter 2 – Customer perceptions and expectations.
Session 7	**Communicating with Customers:** Chapter 4 – Adding a persuasive element. **Cybermarketing:** Chapter 7 – Promoting yourself online, Chapter 8 – Producing your promotional materials online.
Session 8	No specific additional reading.
Session 9	**Effective Communication:** Chapter 5 – The power of persuasion, Chapter 9 – Adverts, news releases and displays.
Session 10	No specific additional reading.
Session 11	No specific additional reading.
Session 12	**Effective Communication:** Chapter 14 – Future communication: the role of technology. **Cybermarketing:** Chapter 9 – E-commerce: selling online, Chapter 10 – Where is all this taking us?

Table 4 – Marketing models

The text in the Companion Sessions refers to appropriate models and concepts or assumes knowledge but does not reproduce these, as they can be seen in the core textbooks for Certificate level. Useful references from the core text for Marketing Fundamentals are supplied in the following table. Please note that this does not necessarily represent the full range of models that you will need to study for your exam or assessment.

Session	Marketing Model	Reference: Dibb, Simkin, Pride & Ferrell: *Marketing – concepts and strategies* – 4th European Edition – Houghton Mifflin
Session 1	■ Marketing concept.	■ Page 9.
Session 2	■ No specific models.	
Session 3	■ Communication process. ■ Graphical presentation of information. ■ Graphical presentation of information.	■ Page 456. ■ Page 706. ■ Page 214.
Session 4	■ No specific models.	
Session 5	■ Nature of customer complaints.	■ Page 114.
Session 6	■ Consumer buying decision process. ■ B2b buying/relationships.	■ Page 109. ■ Page 153/154.
Session 7	■ Using promotional tools. ■ Elements of personal selling. ■ Sales promotions.	■ Page 459. ■ Page 524. ■ Page 542.

Session	Marketing Model	Reference: Dibb, Simkin, Pride & Ferrell: *Marketing concepts and strategies* – 4th European Edition – Houghton Mifflin
Session 8	■ Building awareness. ■ Topics for press releases. ■ Expenditure on sponsorship.	■ Page 460/461. ■ Page 509. ■ Page 514.
Session 9	■ Advertising campaign planning. ■ Advertising media. ■ Elements of artwork. ■ Advertisement techniques. ■ AIDA. ■ Direct mail industry. ■ Growth in direct marketing. ■ Ethics of advertising.	■ Page 489. ■ Page 496/498. ■ Page 500/501. ■ Page 502. ■ Page 499. ■ Page 546. ■ Page 554. ■ Page 763.
Session 10	■ No specific models.	
Session 11	■ Brand equity. ■ Logo. ■ Family branding.	■ Page 273. ■ Page 278. ■ Page 280.
Session 12	■ No specific models.	

Session 1

Organisations and stakeholders

Introduction

It is important that organisations and marketers understand the concept of the customer, so this Session explores this and differentiates between the different types of customers. In today's competitive environment, knowledge of the customer and how to meet or exceed their needs is a significant factor in being able to gain competitive advantage. Developing effective customer relationships is discussed in detail in the next Session, but the principles of customer focus and relationship marketing are examined below.

LEARNING OUTCOMES

At the end of this Session you will be able to:

- Appreciate organisations as open systems.
- Explain what is meant by the terms 'customer', 'stakeholder' and 'user'.
- Demonstrate the fundamental importance of customers to all forms of organisations, including services and the need to identify them clearly.
- Describe the link between the marketing concept, customer focus, and relationship marketing.
- Distinguish between internal and external customers.
- Appreciate the need for effective internal and external customer communication and their link to, and role in maintaining, customer focus – in order to develop and sustain good customer relations.

The organisation as an open system

A business organisation is an open system (not a closed system that is self-sufficient) because it interacts with its environment. Within an organisation there are a number of different parts which are all inter-related, so what happens in one area impacts on another.

As an open system, the organisation receives inputs from outside, and processes them in order to produce an output as illustrated in Figure 1.1.

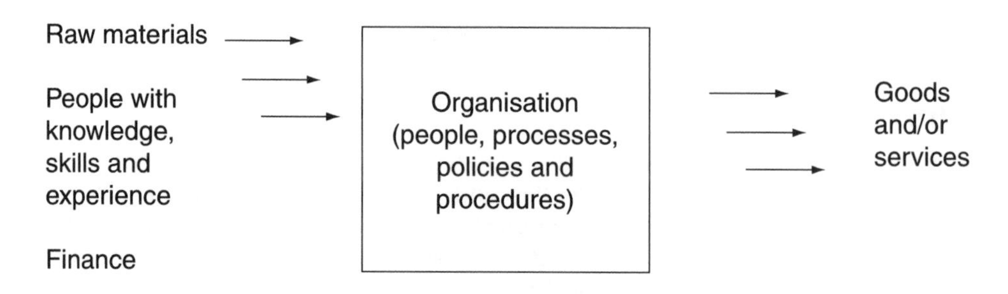

Figure 1.1: The organisation as an open system

Therefore what happens in the environment may impact to a greater or lesser degree on the organisation, depending on the nature of its business. The marketer uses tools such as LEPEST (Legal, Economic, Political, Environmental, Social, Technical) to help identify the environmental forces that may impact on the organisation.

Determining a response requires the gathering and analysing of other information such as current organisation strengths and weaknesses and competitor activity. In some situations the organisation is forced to respond, such as in complying with new industry regulations. In other circumstances it may choose whether to do so or not. For example, when the customer needs change, the organisation may decide to modify or develop a new product to meet the new requirements or leave the market to rivals who are more able.

Stakeholders

These are individuals or groups who affect the organisation or who are affected by some aspect of the organisation. Therefore they include shareholders and employees, customers and suppliers – i.e. they may be internal or external to the organisation. They may have conflicting requirements or expectations of the organisation. For example, customers will want to pay as little as possible for the organisation's goods and services while suppliers will want to be paid as much as possible! The organisation has to balance carefully the needs of all the stakeholders. Figure 1. 2 identifies the main stakeholder groups and individuals.

Figure 1.2: An organisation's stakeholders

It can be appreciated that the organisation needs to communicate with its stakeholders. The messages must be consistent and co-ordinated so that each group understands the fundamental purpose of the organisation and its values. However, the content and medium chosen must be relevant to the groups concerned. Obviously some messages are universal (image, policies, branding) whilst others will be sent to a specific group.

There are many different ways in which organisations communicate with stakeholders, including sponsorship activities, exhibitions and events, newsletters, brochures, advertisements, logo, packaging, catalogues, letters, memos, faxes and emails. You will explore these in some depth in later Sessions in this Companion.

Activity 1.1: Communicating with stakeholders

As the Marketing Manager for a company that recycles waste paper you are concerned that your stakeholders are fully aware of the environmentally friendly policies that the company operates. How can this message be communicated as widely as possible? Brainstorm this with fellow students and colleagues.

Identifying customers

Marketers are told that it is important to understand the customer so they can identify needs and find ways of meeting these. Therefore, it is important to know who the customers are, because they are not simply the people who buy your organisation's products and services.

It is fairly easy to identify the external customer but what about the internal customer – the person working in the organisation who receives a product or service from someone else working in the organisation? From this it can be seen that there is a customer chain that goes across the organisation many times.

In addition, the customer who buys the product may not be the consumer or user of that product, so the customer chain extends beyond the organisation. Manufacturers may sell to wholesalers, who sell to retailers who sell to customers such as parents, who have purchased a product (a toy for example) for their children.

From the above it can be appreciated that the organisation needs to communicate with a wide range of people, groups, other organisations etc. – they are all customers. The following list identifies the different types of customer.

- Purchaser.
- Consumer or user/end-user.
- Initiator – raises awareness of a product or service purchase requirement, perhaps after receiving some promotional material.
- Influencer – affects the purchase in some way, perhaps by persuading the buyer to purchase a particular brand or pay a premium price for perceived added value.
- Gatekeeper – controls the flow of information into an organisation so can prevent purchase if vital information is passed to the right person in time.
- Decision maker.
- Stakeholder.

These customers are all part of what is called the decision making unit or DMU. We will return to the DMU in more detail in Session 6.

In the consumer market the number of different types of customer involved in a purchase is usually limited. For example, a car sale may simply involve a customer and salesperson, although there may also be an initiator and influencer. For example, a parent buying a family car is influenced by other members of the family.

In the business to business (b2b) market is it much more common for the seller to be dealing with a greater number of different individuals and groups over a much longer time period. The sale of a new telecommunications system to an organisation would involve initiators and influencers who raise awareness of the need and what is wanted, and a gatekeeper who may be the personal assistant to the decision maker. The telecommunications company would go through periods of consultation and negotiation with the organisation, via their salespeople and technical experts, to help them identify exactly what was required and how those needs could be met. The organisation would need to survey its staff to identify first their needs. Each individual and group requires information – the telecommunications company needs to communicate with them in some way – directly or indirectly.

What is a customer called?

Organisations do not always refer to their customers by this term. For example, hospitals have patients, radio stations have listeners and cinemas have audiences. Different forms of communication are used to communicate with them. When planning communications the needs of the receiver should be a prime consideration. The needs of patients are different from audiences and listeners.

What examples can you think of?

The importance of customers

Organisations need customers to buy their products and services. For most service organisations the customer and consumer are the same person, since the service is consumed at the point of delivery. So customers are essential for the process to take place. Manufacturers can produce products without the customer being present, but they still need to have a ready market for the goods that they make, because stockpiling is too expensive. If most of their money were tied up in storage, many manufacturers would cease trading fairly quickly. All organisations need people to buy, to ensure a steady flow of cash into their businesses so that they can pay suppliers and employees.

Customers also provide the organisation with information via gathered feedback about their needs and wants, level of satisfaction, changing requirements and reasons for not purchasing and how they want the organisation to communicate with them. This in turn helps the organisation make well-informed decisions about future strategy, operations and tactics.

In b2b markets (business to business markets, sometimes referred to as organisational markets) the organisation's representative or salesperson may speak to a number of different people who initiate and influence purchase before the product is sold for use by another party in the buyer's company.

Buyer behaviour and decision making is discussed in Session 6.

Activity 1.2: Customer chain

Draw a simple diagram to show the customer chain for a bottle of wine from grower to consumer.

The marketing concept

Customers are the focus of attention for marketing oriented companies because they are intent upon identifying and meeting their customer needs in a profitable and efficient way.

Not every organisation is marketing oriented. Some concentrate their energies on product, sales and production.

Production oriented companies favour efficiency and productivity over gaining a greater understanding of what the customer wants.

A product oriented company believes that a good product will sell itself. However, even the highest quality, lowest priced, most innovative product will struggle to gain market share if it is not required by consumers!

An organisation that is sales oriented relies on its salespeople to sell its products. However, if you have ever been persuaded to buy something that you didn't really need, you will appreciate that a company relying on this technique alone will find it difficult to build customer loyalty. Victims of an aggressive sales technique are very reluctant to return. In addition, dissatisfied customers do not refer others and may recommend friends and colleagues not to purchase from a specific organisation that has let them down.

Most organisations recognise how important customers are. US based organisation, Southwest Airlines remind their staff how important each time they receive a pay cheque. These are marked, "From our customers"! Marketing oriented companies concentrate on identifying customer needs and finding ways to satisfy and delight customers. Customer loyalty is important because research shows that the longer a customer remains with you, the more money they will spend with you. They may even become ambassadors for your products and services, referring other people.

Developing a customer-focused culture requires constant reinforcing throughout the organisation. Everyone in the organisation must put the customer (internal and external) and their needs first – the message is to 'think customer' at all times. Internal marketing is essential – this covers the activities and communication that the organisation carries out to create the environment that encourages people to "put the customer first".

The competitive environment encourages organisations to become more customer-focused and seek new ways to retain customers. This impacts on core skills. Marketing oriented organisations need people who listen to their customers, are energised to solve customer problems and are able to ensure that service standards are maintained and improved to meet and beat the competition.

Activity 1.3: Customers first!

Visit your favourite web sites and identify the points that indicate customer focus. For example: How easy is it to navigate? What added value is provided? – extra services, links, etc.

Relationship marketing

Relationship marketing takes the concept of customer focus one step further in that organisations adopting this approach develop marketing practices that encourage customer loyalty. They make every effort to keep in touch with the customer, compile huge databases of customer information and try to find ways of establishing a one-to-one relationship with their most profitable customers.

Customer care also demands that organisations develop relationships with their customers, but this is one that is based on meeting needs at every point of contact. It applies to internal and external customers because employees cannot be expected to look after customers if they are not cared for themselves!

Developing positive customer relationships and Customer Relationship Management (CRM) is explored further in the next Session and in Session 5, which examines how organisations develop effective customer care internally and externally.

Activity 1.4: Is there a problem?

As the Marketing Manager for a large customer service organisation, you have just read the following editorial that appeared in *Marketing Business,* April 2000:

'A survey by Initiative Software (only one of many reaching similar conclusions) has found that British businesses are failing to provide effective Customer Relationship Management programmes (CRM) – and that's if they have one at all. The main problem is that they are not equipping staff with the necessary access to information needed to satisfy the enquiries of those heartless, yet desirable, customers.

Surprisingly or not, the average call handler's parrot-like speech and refusal to go the extra mile is more likely to be down to lack of information than lack of willingness to help. According to the research, call centre telephone operators are unable to provide effective customer relationship management because they not only have inadequate information about customers, but also about their company.'

Write a memo to the Training Manager to request that planned product knowledge training for new staff is prepared and delivered as soon as possible.

Case Study – PC World

Mike Adams, Chief Operating Officer of marketing consultancy Knowledge Accelerators, says, "Too many technology companies are product oriented and not customer oriented, but to survive in the future, they're going to have to turn that way of thinking on its head."

One technology retail company which is coming round to that way of thinking is PC World. Having not enjoyed the greatest reputation for its after-sales service in the past, the Dixons Group retailer is now placing new emphasis on helping customers after the point of sale. An example is its PC performance service, a package which costs the customer more, but provides valuable ongoing support, such as an annual 'healthcheck' where an engineer services the PC to optimise its performance.

PC World is thinking of launching an additional service package, designed to help people install their PCs immediately after sale. This concept has already taken off in France, where it is provided by Mosaic Technology. Called Home Coach, you get an engineer who will come to your home, set up your new PC, get you started on the Internet and email, and configure it to your liking. Mosaic is about to launch this service in the UK.

John Naylor, PC World's Sales Manager, says the retailer's similar service, branded as First Call, should save it substantial sums by reducing the number of calls from confused novices to its contact centre. He says increased levels of after-sales service like these are needed because PC ownership has extended beyond the original group of IT-literate 'techies' into the general population. "We now have a situation where we have products getting more complicated, and then falling into the hands of people with less sophisticated knowledge of technology. That can only mean that there is more demand for tuition-based services."

Interestingly, PC World sees its push into after-sales service as a good opportunity to cross-sell other products into its customer base, demonstrating that brands have much to gain from building ongoing customer relationships.

Source: *Marketing Business,* April 2001.

Questions

1. What evidence is there in the Case Study that PC World are focused on the needs of their customers?
2. What suggestions can you make to help PC World identify the future needs of their customers?
3. What benefits do they expect to gain from introducing First Call?

SUMMARY OF KEY POINTS

- Organisations communicate with a wide range of individuals, groups and other organisations in the course of their business – these are all customers.
- The stakeholders of an organisation are those who affect it or who are affected by the organisation.
- The customer who purchases a product may not be the user or consumer of that product.
- Marketing oriented companies focus on the customer and find effective and efficient ways of meeting their needs.
- Organisations that adopt the relationship marketing approach develop marketing practices that encourage customer loyalty.
- Customer care is about meeting and/or exceeding customer expectations at each point of contact – a key consideration for customer focused organisations.

Improving and developing own learning

The following projects are designed to help you to develop your knowledge and skills further by carrying out some research yourself. Feedback is not provided for this type of learning because there are no 'answers' to be found, but you may wish to discuss your findings with colleagues and fellow students.

Project A

For your organisation, or one you know well, identify:

i) Customers.

ii) Stakeholders.

How effectively does the organisation communicate with each group or individual?

Project B

Consider your own organisation, or one that you know well, and explore what they do to encourage and sustain a customer focused environment.

Consider the extent to which market and customer research is carried out and how that information is used to improve the way the organisation meets customer requirements.

For example, how have products and services been developed over the past five years?

What improvements have been made in response to changing customer needs or identified customer dissatisfaction?

How effectively are customer complaints dealt with?

Does the organisation learn from the experience?

Project C

Carry out some research among friends and colleagues on the organisations that have developed an effective customer relationship with them in order to encourage loyalty.

How was this done?

Why do they remain loyal to that organisation?

Feedback on activities

Activity 1.1: Communicating with stakeholders

Your list may have included some or all of the following – and many more!

- Using recycled material for stationery, packaging, printed promotional material etc.
- Making environmental concerns (events, open days, displays at public events etc.) newsworthy so that news releases result in good media coverage.
- Communicating concern for environment through sponsorship – what opportunities exist for your organisation?

- Communicating internally through newsletters, bulletins, posters etc.
- Gathering information from front-line staff and others on customer response to the organisation's reputation to gauge public awareness, and acting upon the information gathered.
- Monitoring policy compliance at all events such as exhibitions, conferences and new product launches.
- Annual report posted on web site/sent to shareholders.
- Web site.

Activity 1.2: Customer chain

A simple chain may begin with the grower at the vineyard supplying the winemaker with the grapes required to make the wine. The winemaker then sells to the supermarket buyer so the wine goes on sale on the supermarket shelves. From there it is purchased by a customer who serves it at a dinner party to three additional consumers.

At all points the supplier needs to understand the customers' requirements and find ways to meet these. For example, the winemaker will require a certain type of grape of the right quality, in specific quantities and at the right times, to keep the manufacturing process going.

Activity 1.3: Customers first!

The factors that you should be looking for are:

- Ease of navigation and user-friendly layout, so it is easy to find what you need.
- Interesting text with minimum graphics, that require significant time to download.
- Helpful information and advice that is clear and concise.
- Additional web links that are relevant and provide further information.
- Ability to contact organisation, give feedback or interact.
- Consistent quality.
- Credibility.
- Evidence that you – the customer – are important to them and valued highly.

Activity 1.4: Is there a problem?

Customer Focus PLC

Memorandum

To: Brad Courtney
Training Manager

Date: 12 September 200X

From: Gail Knowle
Marketing Manager

Copy: Dee Scott
Customer Services Manager

Subject: Product Knowledge Training

Further to our recent discussions regarding the forthcoming training, I have reviewed our current levels of service and wish to put a top priority on this training.

On examining our customer complaints results I note that an increasing number are due to lack of product knowledge which I believe will be addressed by the training programme you have designed. Therefore, I would like to start this next month, instead of the following month, and try to put everyone through by the end of December.

I realise that this is a very ambitious schedule and understand that you may have some difficulty in meeting this. I propose that we meet to discuss this as soon as possible and will telephone you on 14th September to arrange a time that is convenient for both of us.

In the meantime, please email me if you have any immediate concerns.

Session 2

Developing positive customer relationships

Introduction

This Session follows on from the previous one by considering the importance of effective relationship marketing and appropriate marketing practices. With so much choice available to customers today, most organisations recognise that customer loyalty is of paramount importance, but find it difficult to achieve in a competitive environment. Some of the many factors that influence the methods used by organisations to communicate internally and externally are also explored.

This Session should be studied in conjunction with Session 5, which discusses how to manage customer care.

LEARNING OUTCOMES

At the end of this Session you will be able to:

- Explain why organisations need to develop effective ways of communicating with internal and external customers.
- Discuss how effective communications are linked to customer focus and developing and sustaining good customer relations.
- Discuss what is meant by relationship marketing, and discuss how effective communications contribute to customer loyalty and retention.
- Demonstrate an understanding of how ICT is used in customer service, through the use of databases.

Developing a culture to support customer focus

The previous Session emphasised the importance of involving everyone in the organisation in identifying and meeting customer needs in order to develop a culture of customer care. Some organisations concentrate training on front-line staff who interface directly with the external customer. Others introduce complex policies and procedures and rely on these to ensure that a consistent service is provided to customers.

Many years ago, Marks & Spencer gained a reputation for identifying the importance of internal customer care – 'look after your staff and they will look after the customer'. For service organisations – from banks to office cleaners – this is of paramount importance because in many ways they are 'only as good as their people'. Internal marketing is therefore as important as activities that organisations use to communicate with external customers. Employees need to understand the vision and values of the organisation so they can work within these and promote them externally. For example, if a company value is 'consistency and fairness to all' then this must apply internally, otherwise staff will be unlikely to apply it externally.

Activity 2.1: Actions for customer service

Read the previous Session and carry out some research amongst your fellow students, friends and colleagues to help you write a list of actions that organisations can undertake to ensure that good customer service is part of their prevailing culture.

Methods of communication

Selecting appropriate ways to communicate with internal and external customers can be more challenging than you think. The digital age has led to people receiving more and more information, much of it unsolicited and a significant amount that is not relevant to them. The following table outlines some of the most common forms of communication and major uses.

Method of communication	Internal uses	External uses
Newsletter.	Company successes focusing on internal news and people, raising awareness of vision and values.	Company successes and performance, raising awareness of vision and values.
Annual report.	Company performance, future strategies.	Company performance, future strategies.
Web site.		Company background, catalogue, promotion, selling products and services.
Intranet.	Used as a local network for company documents, papers, policies and procedures. Minutes of meetings may be circulated via the company intranet – password protected.	Internal only – but some organisations make part of their Intranet available externally to suppliers so they can check stock levels etc. This is a company Extranet.

Brochure.	May be used to provide information on pension schemes, training courses etc.	Detailed information on product and services. Usually contains relevant information on the company to build consumer confidence.
Catalogue.	May be used internally for promotional purposes.	Promoting products and services, giving information of range and prices.
Leaflet/Flyer.	May be used internally for promotional purposes.	Product and service promotion.
Letter.	Formal news such as salary increases.	To confirm details, communicate news, reply to letters or complaints, promote products and services.
Email.	For short, speedy and simple messages – ideal form of internal communication.	For short, speedy and simple messages.
Memo.	For short, speedy and simple messages – ideal form of internal communication when more permanent record is required than email; is also more formal than email.	Rarely used due to its relative informal nature.
Fax.	For short, speedy and simple messages when separated by distance and time.	For short, speedy and simple messages when separated by distance and time.
Telephone.	For discussion, to make arrangements etc. when an immediate answer or personal approach is required. Email has taken over from telephone to a large extent internally.	For discussion, to make arrangements etc. when an immediate answer or personal approach is required.

Meetings and briefings.	Meetings used to gather and disseminate information, solve problems and make decisions. Daily and weekly briefings used to pass on information about progress, people, problems etc.	Meetings used to gather and disseminate information, solve problems and make decisions. Briefings rarely used.
Marketing activities and promotions.	Internal communications on the organisation, what it stands for, benefits for employees etc.	To promote products and services to consumers, establish corporate identity and communicate company vision and values.
Branding and packaging.	Establish and build brand so staff can communicate this externally.	Establish and build brand; packaging used to protect and promote product.

Figure 2.1: Communicating with internal and external customers

The above are discussed in more detail throughout this Companion.

Communicating effectively with people and making sure they are provided with the right information at the right time, or know how to access it, is key to establishing good working relationships internally and externally. For example, if suppliers understand the business of the organisation and its problems, they help look for solutions to problems. Within the organisation, people should be encouraged to share ideas on how to improve customer service by looking for more cost-effective or quicker ways of meeting needs. Internal and external customers are more likely to be loyal to an organisation that uses two-way communication to help solve problems and build stronger relationships. The large supermarket giants such as Sainsbury's, Tesco and Safeway have developed shopping trolleys with special baby and toddler seats to make shopping at their store easier and safer for busy parents with children.

The importance of effective two-way communication

By now you will appreciate that many of the communications that organisations make are intended to be two-way as opposed to one-way. For example, in meetings very little would be achieved if people did not participate, share ideas and listen to others. In contrast, briefings are mainly a one-way communication, used as noted above, to pass on information. Unlike meetings, questions are confined to the end of the communication and limited to ensuring understanding of the information, not discussion.

Organisations need to develop effective ways of communicating with all types of customers in order to identify their needs, check that they are satisfying those needs and to find out how customer needs will change in the future. Once the relationship has been established, it needs to be maintained. Organisations need to find ways of doing this through appropriate communications and contact. A good example of this is given in the Case Study at the end of this Session.

Activity 2.2: Web links

As the Manager of a football club you are assessing the potential benefits of the corporate web site prior to further investment. Write a bulleted list of the potential advantages for:

i) The organisation.

ii) The fans.

Why customer loyalty is important

True loyalty exists when the customer exhibits the desire to continue using an organisation as a supplier of products and services. On the way to this there may be different stages of loyalty when the customer buys but does not feel any particular loyalty so may switch suppliers if they look around. Customers may also be loyal to more than one supplier. For example, we may not always purchase petrol from the same garage or eat at the same restaurant when we go out, but purchase frequently enough to be described as a valuable and loyal customer.

Loyal customers provide many benefits for organisations:

- They are easier to do business with because there is a degree of mutual needs existing between the two parties.

- They tend to spend more.
- They act as ambassadors.
- They recommend specific products and services to others.
- Research shows that it costs at least five times more to recruit a new customer than to keep an existing one.

The above holds for b2b and business to consumer (b2c) markets. However, the nature of relationships in b2b markets, where personal selling is used more commonly to sell complex products, means that the length of time between initial interest or enquiry to placing the order is longer than in most consumer transactions. This gives the salesperson and his or her organisation more contact time and opportunity to start building a relationship that might last beyond the first purchase. By the time the order is placed, both parties hold a great deal of information about each other and should have some idea of whether the relationship is likely to be sustained.

Factors affecting customer loyalty include:

- Price – customers are lured away by special offers or cheaper prices elsewhere.
- Service – poor quality service at some point of contact is likely to cause dissatisfaction; sometimes the organisation will find out and have the chance to make good their mistake; sometimes customers simply turn to competitors.
- Product – the product no longer meets their needs.
- Lack of need – they no longer have a requirement for the product or service.
- Organisation's image – the customer no longer wishes to be associated with the organisation for some reason, such as poor social responsibility record for example.
- Accessibility – a new channel, such as the Internet, makes it easier to obtain the product.

Factors that contribute to the development of customer loyalty include the opposite of the examples given above. Satisfied customers tend to return but organisations cannot expect this in a competitive environment. A major factor in developing loyalty is the ability of the organisation to develop a relationship with the customer that is built on understanding of needs.

Activity 2.3: Measuring customer satisfaction

Satisfied customers are more likely to sustain a relationship with an organisation and continue to buy. What methods could be used to measure customer satisfaction by:

i) A retail organisation?

ii) A bank?

Developing customer loyalty

Most of us are familiar with loyalty programmes and schemes introduced by organisations to tie customers into a relationship. One of the most widely used is the loyalty card. Through purchasing products the customer collects 'points' which can be exchanged for money-off vouchers or gifts. The majority of the large supermarkets have been operating these types of scheme for some time. Other loyalty schemes involve offering free 'membership' which entitles 'members' to special offers and discounts.

The organisation operating the loyalty scheme must carefully measure the quantitative benefits of customer loyalty against the cost of running the scheme. Costs include the cost of the discounts offered, paperwork and administration. To help carry out this type of analysis information must be collected on:

- Frequency of purchase.
- Value of purchase.
- Date of last purchase.
- Type of purchase.

Research shows that loyal customers are more likely to respond to communications and that those purchasing in the recent past are more likely to repeat buy than a customer who has not entered into a transaction with the organisation for more than two years.

However, the latest research is showing that loyalty cards are perhaps not having the desired effect. Supermarkets are finding that customers are still shopping elsewhere, despite having a loyalty card.

Customer databases

Compiling and maintaining a customer database – see Case Study – is essential if organisations are to communicate effectively with customers. The database stores data on customer preferences and purchase patterns that enables marketers to identify target groups of customer for specific promotions. A car dealership send direct mailings to carefully selected customers – those who have demonstrated an interest in such products and who are most likely to purchase a new car – when new models are launched. Without the information from the database only a blanket mailing is possible, resulting in a costly waste of the promotional budget.

Case Study – I want a relationship

Central to the idea of CRM is the concept of treating each customer as an individual and using the knowledge a company has of a customer to talk sensibly to them, communicating offers they are likely to be interested in and not wasting their time with offers that don't meet their needs. This knowledge is held, in an ideal world, on one centralised database, which anyone in the company can interrogate for their own department's ends.

It goes without saying then, that for CRM to work, the quality of the database is all. Yet as Duncan Painter, General Manager of Sand Technologies Europe, which has developed the Nucleus set of data warehousing tools, point out, companies are sometimes so preoccupied with pulling the database together that they don't stop to think about the sort of data they require.

"The key thing is to understand what the source data is that they really need to obtain to populate these environments and also, do they really understand what customer value and customer relationships are?" he says. Without the right information on customers, such as their payment record and how much servicing the customer's account needs, Painter argues it's impossible to mine the data to produce any meaningful results.

Equally important, once the database has been created, is to keep it fresh, according to Alistair Bremmer, UK Managing Director of Saratoga Systems, the developer of the Avenue CRM software suite. "In order to make the full capital on a CRM system, the field force needs to take that data with them in a usable form, revise it, add to it, and then come back to the mother ship and synchronise in a capable fashion," says Bremmer. "All too often, the CRM vendors out there are building the panacea, but that panacea needs an aircraft carrier to sit alongside it."

This ability to update customer data regularly and rapidly has become even more important, of course, as companies and their customers communicate through an increasing number of channels, from traditional above- and below-the-line media to call centres, interactive television and the Internet. When it comes to choosing the data warehousing tools to analyse and interrogate the database, each package has its own capabilities and the vendors, of course, will be more than happy to demonstrate them.

But whatever the merits of any given package, James Wilson, Worldwide Reporting Infrastructure Manager for enterprise services at Sun Microsystems, who is heavily involved in data exploitation and has assessed many CRM packages, advises prospective CRM purchasers to try out their intended CRM solutions in 'real-world' situations.

"Get an example of what you want the system to do and get the company supplying the software to demonstrate that example on the same volume of data that it will be required to work on in your company," he says. "Too often companies commit to licensing software without truly testing it, and then suffer in the long run."

Stewart Holness, Vice President, e-commerce, at MicroStrategy draws a distinction between customer relationship management systems, which track all interactions between a company and a customer, and the customer relationship management systems that his company has developed, which market a company's products and services to customers in a way that puts the customer in control of when and how they are marketed to. MicroStrategy's systems sit on top of a data warehouse or CRM system and enable companies to set up a relationship with a consumer so that the consumer can subscribe and receive alerts or scheduled information that is pertinent to them.

A typical MicroStrategy customer is Blockbuster Video, which uses the system to mine databases and ask consumers to register the type of film they like by segment, theme or age group. It then makes personalised automated calls or sends emails in the afternoon, offering the customer the option to reserve a film which it thinks they will like – based on the preferences they have expressed – for collection in their local store later that day.

"The critical component is that it's based on conditions that the consumer controls; it's the obverse of spamming," says Holness. "The consumer can turn it off; the consumer sets the thresholds and triggers, and controls the rules. From the company's perspective, they are not just spamming people who have signalled no interest."

Applications such as this show the potential power of customer relationship management and marketing systems. But as Sand's Duncan Painter cautions, companies would do well not to get too carried away with the technology.

"CRM is as much a cultural change to a company as it is a technology change," he says. "Too often, people charge into technology solutions before they've answered, or even asked, the right questions."

Source: *Marketing Business,* March 2000.

Questions

1. What examples can you find in the Case Study that indicates that many organisations are not very skilled at building effective relationships with customers?
2. What advice does James Wilson give to prospective purchaser of CRM systems?
3. Why do you think that Duncan Painter describes CRM as a cultural change as much as a technology change?

SUMMARY OF KEY POINTS

- Everyone in the organisation needs to take responsibility for developing a prevailing culture of excellence in customer service and customer focus.
- Developing effective long-term customer relationships requires that organisations understand how to meet current and future needs and regularly communicate to ensure ongoing satisfaction.
- Customer loyalty is developed over time by communicating regularly and meeting needs.
- Loyal customers are important because they tend to spend more over time and recommend others.

- Many factors influence customer loyalty including price, product benefits and customer service levels.
- CRM systems need to be developed to meet an organisation's needs and tested in the organisation's 'real world' before purchase.
- The data stored on customer databases can be used to identify target groups of customers for specific promotions.

Improving and developing own learning

The following projects are designed to help you to develop your knowledge and skills further by carrying out some research yourself. Feedback is not provided for this type of learning because there are no 'answers' to be found but you may wish to discuss your findings with colleagues and fellow students.

Project A

Identify all the ways organisations communicate with internal and external customers. Collect as many examples as you can.

What do you think is the purpose of each?

How well has that objective been achieved through the communication?

Project B

Which organisations have taken time to establish and build a long-term relationship with you as a customer? For each of these consider:

i) How has this been achieved by the organisation through communicating with you?

ii) What factors have led to this relationship being sustained over a period of time?

iii) How loyal do you think you are to that organisation, products/services and brands?

iv) What would influence you to change to a rival organisation for the same products and services?

Project C

Consider your favourite charities and the methods they use to communicate with you – for example, telephone or letter.

How do they attempt to involve you and encourage your loyalty?

How successful is this?

If you were a fund-raiser for a charity, what use would you make of a customer database?

Feedback on activities

Activity 2.1: Actions for customer service

- Ensure everyone in the organisation receives **appropriate** customer care training. Managers need skills to help them manage customer care through others, while front-line staff require skills training to enable them to interact effectively with external customers and solve their problems. Senior Managers need to understand how to develop effective customer care strategies and respond effectively to customer feedback.
- Ensure customer care training is kept up to date!

- Empower front-line staff so they can make decisions that will solve customer problems on the spot, rather than having to go to a higher authority. An example might be giving restaurant staff the discretion to replace a drink free of charge if it is knocked over by the customer.
- Gather customer feedback and respond appropriately. There are many ways of collecting such information:
  - Survey carried out face to face, over the telephone, by email or by mailshot.
  - Mystery shopper – many retail companies use this method to test their people and processes.
  - Talk to front-line staff because they talk – and listen – directly to customers. In fact they may be the only person in the company that the dissatisfied customer does communicate with. Many such customers do not complain – they just never return, so the company may never know what went wrong.
  - Collect information from customers on the company web site, via a 'contact us' button or feedback form.
  - Make it easy for customers to complain – if it is not easy, customers with a grievance will not bother to give the company a second chance.
- Have a bias for action – many organisations collect customer feedback and analyse it, but then do very little.
- Review customer care procedures on a regular basis and use employees from all levels in the organisation to make suggestions for improvements.
- Recognise and reward excellence in customer service throughout the organisation, and communicate successes via posters, noticeboards and company newsletters.
- Communicate the ethos of customer service throughout the organisation as above, and externally via newsletters and PR activities.

Activity 2.2: Web links

Potential benefits for the organisation include:

- Online booking – reduced administration costs compared to telephone and face to face booking.
- Advertising and promotion platform.
- Online sales facilities for merchandise etc.

- Greater access to customer feedback.
- Opportunity to develop brand.
- Faster communication channels – negative messages can be responded to instantly, while positive messages can be reinforced.
- Opportunity to communicate directly with fans – message is not 'reinterpreted' by the media.
- Opportunity to gain competitive advantage – better facilities, more user-friendly site, etc.

Potential benefits for the club fans include:

- Information on team players (backgrounds, profiles etc.), history of the club and its achievements.
- Current information about forthcoming games.
- Online booking.
- Improved customer service through more efficient and streamlined booking facility.
- Reviews of previous games.
- Catalogue of branded merchandise.
- Online purchase of merchandise.
- Ability to put questions to team players/Managers.
- Interaction with other fans.
- Information about membership of fan clubs and similar.
- Search facility for quick access to information required and club archives.
- Feedback facility.
- Current news releases.

Activity 2.3: Measuring customer satisfaction

i) A retail organisation might use a mystery shopper, telephone or postal survey if the purchase were a large item such as a computer; or questionnaire at point of sale.

ii) A bank is most likely to use a telephone survey or gather feedback via the Internet from customers who i-bank (bank over the Internet). Valuable customers may have a personal banker assigned to them who will keep in touch to assess ongoing satisfaction and to introduce new products and services that would provide additional benefits.

Session 3

The communication process

Introduction

This Session explores what is meant by effective communication, and shows how to plan successful communications. It includes a review of personal selling, telephone technique and a discussion on body language and the non-verbal clues we send in face to face situations. Barriers to effective communication are also examined.

In the final sections you will explore how to produce business and marketing communications such as reports and notices, review how to interpret and summarise and learn how to present written and graphical information. This Session should be studied in conjunction with all other Sessions that cover alternative strategies for communicating with different stakeholder groups.

It is the longest Session in the Companion as the different communication methods are explored in some detail.

LEARNING OUTCOMES

At the end of this Session you will be able to:

- Explain the structure and function of the communication process.
- Explain the communications planning process to produce effective strategies for improving alternative communications formats.
- Explain the advantages and disadvantages of oral communications in different face to face situations.
- Discuss the communication process involved in personal selling.
- Discuss what is meant by good telephone technique.
- Explain the importance of effective body language in face to face situations and describe strategies to improve non-verbal communication skills.
- Discuss how to improve listening skills.
- Describe how to plan effective communications.
- Identify barriers to effective communication and how these might be avoided or overcome.
- Consider how to use letters, memoranda, notices, emails and reports when communicating with internal and external customers.
- Interpret, summarise and present written and graphical information.

What is effective communication?

Effective communication can be represented by the following familiar model:

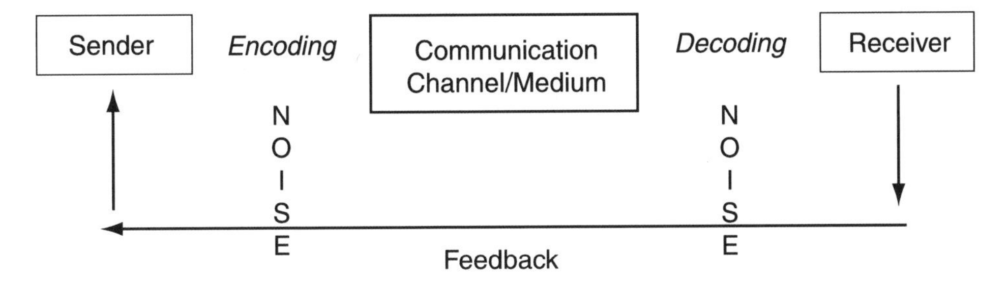

Figure 3.1: Simple model of effective communication

The **Sender** plans the communication and decides the content, channel and format according to the purpose of the communication and the needs of the receiver. For example, in an office, the sender may consider whether to use email or write a memo, which is a more formal means of communicating. He/she will consider how to make the message clear and concise so that the receiver is able to decode or interpret it correctly. This process is called **Encoding** and includes decisions on content and channel.

The **Channel** selected will depend on the type of communication and in the above example would be written memo or email. However, if planning a more complex communication such as an advertising campaign, you might consider television and press media.

The **Receiver** 'lives' in a different world to the sender, so interprets the message according to own knowledge, skills and experience. This process is called **Decoding** and is a major reason for communication breakdown if the message is not clear or if an inappropriate channel is chosen. For example, in the office, for an important message that requires an immediate response and perhaps some discussion, it would be more appropriate to use the telephone so that the immediate response can be delivered, rather than by sending an email.

The disadvantage of telephone is that the receiver has to be present to take part in the discussion. The disadvantage of email is that a series may need to be exchanged before the discussion is concluded, because the lack of personal involvement means that misunderstandings or further questions cannot be dealt with at the time. The sender may not know that the receiver did not understand or have enough information until the next email reply arrives!

Feedback is required by the sender to ensure that the message was correctly interpreted – i.e. the communication was effective. This might be a confirmation, an appropriate reply or observable action in response to the message.

Noise is the name that is given to interference or distractions that prevent effective transmission of the message from sender to receiver. Noise can occur at any point. It includes not only physical interruption but emotional and semantic interference (words) as well. This is discussed further in the next section.

Barriers to effective communication

Barriers to effective communication can be summarised under three headings:

- Physical – can be seen, heard, touched.
- Psychological – related to feelings, emotions.
- Semantic – to do with language, words.

Physical barriers include factors in the immediate environment that prevent people from communicating effectively, such as loud noises and long distances between sender and receiver. A less obvious environmental factor is temperature. Consider the last time you attended a meeting or presentation where the room temperature was too hot or too cold. How did it affect your ability to listen or participate?

Another physical barrier is human disability – how often when you communicate do you consider any special needs the receiver may have? In a noisy shop, some people might find it difficult to hear and be embarrassed to admit to a physical disability, so do not ask for clarification. This could lead to misunderstandings on both sides and result in customer dissatisfaction. The sender must be able to deal with this and also be appropriately skilled and able to send clear and concise messages.

Psychological barriers include emotions such as anger, aggressiveness and shyness. Emotions often prevent clear articulation of the message, which may then become personal and lose meaning. Equally, if the message excites emotion in the receiver then he/she will not decode it effectively. Marketers sometimes use shock tactics when designing advertisements to attract attention, but this might also prevent the real message from being received.

Other psychological barriers include status, intelligence, prejudice and education – people feeling inferior become unable to communicate effectively in some circumstances. It is also difficult to communicate with a disinterested receiver – hence advertisers' rigorous efforts to grab attention.

Semantics includes the words and language used. Written and spoken communications need to be clear, concise and understandable. It is often difficult to know how much information to include – too much and people will lose interest; not enough and they will not understand. Jargon and 'technical-speak' also cause confusion because the receiver may not have the same knowledge as the sender.

When planning communications there are some simple rules to apply:

- Use appropriate language for the target audience and avoid jargon.
- KISS – keep it short and simple.
- Use a channel that means the message will reach the right audience in the right format at the right time.
- Decide whether face to face or telephone is more appropriate than a written message.
- Use the right degree of formality – respond to a letter by letter (or telephone if speed is more important) rather than a less formal email – unless this has been agreed.
- If planning complex written communications, pilot it with a representative group to check understanding.

Activity 3.1: Noise

Advertisements are marketing communications designed to inform, influence or persuade. However, this type of communication is not always effective – people do not always give the right response even if they belong to the target audience. 'Noise' can prevent the message being received.

Consider an advertisement that appears on primetime television. What examples of noise can you think of? Write down your ideas in the form of a bulleted list.

Oral communications

Face to face communication is not always convenient because both sender and receiver need to be in close proximity. Similarly, it is often easier to send a memo or an email than to pick up a telephone, but this imposes constraints on the message that can be transmitted.

Oral communication has the main advantage in that discussion can take place, so both sender and receiver can use appropriate questioning and listening skills to check understanding. The sender is not present when the receiver is interpreting written communication so the words used are very important if misunderstanding is to be avoided. The main advantage of written communication is that the sender has time to prepare the message; it is not spoken and received at the same time. Selecting the right strategy for communication depends of the nature of the message, the speed at which it needs to be transmitted and the number of people that require the same information at the same time.

The main advantages of oral communication compared are summarised in Figure 3.2:

Face to face	Telephone
Sender can observe the effect the message is having on the receiver and can adjust if appropriate.	Observation is not possible – unless using a web phone or tele-conferencing.
Complex messages can be transmitted because understanding can be checked by questioning the receiver. For example, interviewers carrying out marketing research can ask more complicated questions than would be appropriate for a postal survey.	Complex messages can be transmitted because understanding can be checked by questioning the receiver. For example, interviewers carrying out marketing research can ask more complicated questions than would be appropriate for a postal survey.
Communication is two-way, so ideas and information can be shared and discussed.	Communication is two-way so ideas and information can be shared and discussed.

Personal communication often leads to greater commitment to action. The receiver is committing to a person; not a machine or a piece of paper.	Speaking to a person aids commitment because it is more personal.
The message can be reinforced via body language and tone of voice.	The message can be reinforced via tone of voice.

Figure 3.2: Advantages of oral communication

If communicating simple messages, then written format can be used. It is also the best format to use if disseminating information to a large number of people. Different ways of communicating in writing are discussed in the later Sessions of this Companion.

Activity 3.2: Making contact

Read the following extract from an article that appeared in *Marketing Business,* July/August 2001.

'Statistics from the research company Forrester suggest that as few as 33% of consumers attempting to purchase online do so, and that 90% of online buyers fail to make a repeat purchase.

Byzantium, a UK technology company, believes that part of the problem lies in the fact that online shoppers are left very much to their own devices. The company has spent the last two years developing a solution which aims to bring the human touch to online shopping.

The company's 'Hyphone' system places a button on the web site which users can click when they need help or advice. The Hyphone button puts the user in contact with a call centre agent via text chat or Voice Over Internet Protocol (VOIP), which enables the agent and the user to talk, via the PC, over the same telephone connection that is used to access the web site.

Using the Hyphone, the agent can send any relevant files direct to the user's desktop, or redirect the user to any other page on the Internet. Combined with the interactive chat facility, this is a powerful tool, enabling the call centre agent to suggest an action and then instigate it on the user's behalf.

If the user should experience difficulty filling in forms, he or she can use Hyphone's collaborative form-filling function to turn to the agent for help, or even dictate answers if typing skills are not all they should be. As a security measure, the completed form can only be submitted by the user, not the agent.

If the agent thinks it might be helpful to draw a diagram for the user, he or she can call up a virtual whiteboard, draw the diagram and then put the file onto the user's desktop. At this point, both the agent and the user can amend or annotate the diagram using a set of tools similar to those found in any PC art or design programme.'

Having read the extract, list the advantages of human contact.

Personal selling

Personal selling can be defined as the personal presentation of the company and its products to a customer or prospective customer. There are many situations where organisations feel it is necessary to use this form of promotion, but most often when product complexity is high.

In the b2b market where many sales are of customised products and service, salespeople are used to develop a relationship with the prospective customer, work with them to determine needs, and then find attractive ways to meet those requirements. The communication process is complex and time consuming. The salesperson needs excellent communication skills that include:

- Questioning and listening skills.
- Negotiation skills.
- Assertive communication skills.
- Influencing skills.
- Observation skills.
- Excellent grammar and vocabulary.
- Fluency in language.
- Presentation skills.

The salesperson uses all the above skills as he/she plans appropriate communications during the personal selling process as outlined below.

AIDA	b2b market	b2c market
Attention – this begins pre-sale.	Appointment is made with prospective client, probably via personal assistant. As a formal part of the process, letter and telephone are the most appropriate channels – possibly email if a relationship has already been established. The sales presentation in this market is more complex and formal. Opening words must convince and reassure as well as gain the attention – the salesperson needs to put him/herself in the customer's shoes.	The salesperson must observe the prospective customer and approach when time is right – people need time to browse but must also feel that service is available. Opening words must convince and reassure as well as gain the attention – the salesperson needs to put him/herself in the customer's shoes. Sales presentation is structured as in b2b market but is likely to take up less time.
Interest – sale will be lost if customer is not engaged or does not feel involved.	Careful questioning and listening skills are required to elicit needs. The salesperson must also use open body language and observe the body language of the prospective client to see how the message is being received. If giving a product demonstration, the purpose must be clearly explained so the client knows what is of benefit for him/her.	Careful questioning and listening skills are required to elicit needs. The salesperson must also use open body language and observe that of the prospective customer to see how the message is being received.
Desire – empathy is essential; communication must be clear and concise.	Sell benefits and overcome objectives to create desire in prospective client. Negotiation or bargaining will take place at this stage. LISTEN TO THE PROSPECTIVE CLIENT.	Sell benefits and overcome objectives to create desire in prospective client. There may be some negotiation on price or package. LISTEN TO THE PROSPECTIVE CUSTOMER.
Action – use an effective close.	Close the sale and confirm order. Tell the client what happens next.	Close the sale and confirm order. Tell the customer what happens next.

Figure 3.3: Communication skills used during process of personal selling

Although different skills are mentioned at different stages, they are not exclusive to those stages. Throughout the presentation the salesperson must listen, question and observe effectively in order to respond appropriately. Poor communicators will deliver a set sales pitch without deviation! Effective communicators will make sure they deliver the right information at the right time, but only when the prospect is ready.

Communicating by telephone

Use the following checklists to evaluate how well you communicate on the telephone. For example, do you speak too much so the other person cannot get their point across?

To communicate effectively on the telephone:

- Prepare for the call by making sure you have all the information you need.
- Smile – you will sound more approachable and interested.
- Be friendly but polite and helpful if dealing with enquiries.
- Ask questions to gather information.
- Reflect back so the person at the other end knows you understand.
- Take notes – do not rely on your memory.
- Limit your talking and don't interrupt.
- Concentrate; don't be distracted.
- LISTEN.

To minimise problems on the telephone:

- Answer promptly; people do not like to be kept waiting.
- Pass messages on quickly.
- Call back when you said you would – even if there is no news!
- Use callers' names.
- Don't keep people on hold for too long.
- Apologise if you have to leave the telephone to seek information.
- Explain what will happen next if passing to another department and...
- ...let the next person know who is calling and why.
- Prepare what you are going to say in case you have to leave a message.

When answering the telephone:

- Greet people by name.
- Tell them who you are.
- Ask 'How may I help you,' or similar.
- Act promptly to requests or offer to call back at an agreed time.

Questioning skills

In most customer contact situations you need to identify needs and agree appropriate actions to satisfy these. You will only do this through effective questioning and active listening.

Effective questioning means being able to draw out information, feelings and opinions from the other person. There are several types of question you can use:

OPEN – to gather information. Useful ways to begin open questions are what, why, when, where, how or tell me about…? Open questions should be carefully focused so that they are not too broad; otherwise the respondent may not give an appropriate answer.

Example: How may I help you? ('May I help you' is a closed question, and will receive a yes or no answer). What did you do next?

PROBING – to find out further information or more detail.

Examples: What happened next? How did you find out?

REFLECTIVE – repeat or paraphrase the speaker's last sentence(s) to confirm understanding, especially if they have been explaining an important point that you need to confirm before moving on.

Example: I understand that you have tried to contact the customer service department on three separate occasions by telephone and have not been able to get through?

CLOSED – usually requires a yes or no response.

Example: Do you have your receipt?

LINKING – shows you have been listening and noted an important point made earlier by linking back to it. A useful technique for controlling 'wafflers' or long-winded speakers at meetings!

Example: You mentioned the new marketing project earlier; in what way is this giving you problems?

CLARIFYING – brings the discussion to a particular point and enables the questioner to move on to seek further information. Can be used in a similar way to the linking question.

Example: From your responses, I think that we all agree to attend the Trade Show in April in order to launch the new product; is that correct?

MULTIPLE – avoid asking several questions at the same time because you will confuse.

Example: When you designed the leaflet did you add a money-off coupon, and has it been proofed yet, and when is the final deadline for this?

LEADING – the answer is indicated in the question. Avoid.

Example: I think that it is the right decision to sponsor the art show, don't you?

SILENCE is also a means of drawing someone out. It can show how relaxed you are, and will therefore encourage your respondent to relax. It also makes it clear that it is up to the other person to speak. It is only embarrassing if you allow it to be!

Practice using the appropriate questions in conversation and see what a difference it makes to your ability to communicate effectively.

Listening dynamics

We can hear many more words than a speaker has the ability to say. So while the other person is speaking your brain has capacity to think about something else as well. It's not surprising that people are easily distracted and do not listen attentively all the time. Effective listening is an active process; it is hearing that is passive.

In a positive working relationship the only acceptable listener is an active one. However, not many people make the effort to listen actively at all times. Figure 3.4 compares three different types of listeners. Which one do you tend to be?

Marginal listeners.	■ Tend to be preoccupied with their own thoughts. ■ Stare blankly into space. ■ Insult the speaker by their indifference. ■ Convey a self-centred attitude. ■ Misunderstand more than half of what is said.
Evaluative listeners.	■ Evaluate what is said in their own way rather than trying to listen or understand. ■ Concentrate on composing a response. ■ Make instant judgements about the speaker and what he/she is saying. ■ Finish the speaker's sentences. ■ Rush through a conversation.
Active listeners.	■ Concentrate on what people are saying. ■ Make an effort to see the speaker's viewpoint. ■ Give feedback to the speaker.

Figure 3.4: Three different types of listeners

Developing better listening skills

Try to practise the following to improve your listening skills:

- Resist distractions – ignore external and internal 'noise' and concentrate on the speaker.
- Let people tell their own story – when listening to a problem, let them tell it the way they want to and do not interrupt, in case you miss valuable information. Save your questions for later.
- Take notes – most of us can remember around 50% of what we hear, so take notes to remind you of exactly what was said.
- Listen to everything and try not to screen out what you don't want to hear, or react to negative things that are said. Emotion creates internal 'noise'.
- Give feedback – let the speaker know that you are paying attention by giving verbal and non-verbal "cues", for example by nodding you head or saying "Yes, I understand".
- "Read between the lines" – sometimes the message someone wants to convey is in the part they leave out. Check it out by asking open questions to get more information.
- Show that you care – there is no such thing as an uninteresting speaker, only disinterested listeners!
- SMILE when appropriate and appear interested and alert.
- Ask questions – to check that you have understood.

Non-verbal communication

When speaking in face to face situations we give non-verbal clues, referred to as body language, that transmits messages to the receiver. These are made up of the gestures we make, hand-to-face movements, facial expressions, posture, the way we stand or sit and other actions that we make. These are open to interpretation but there are some commonly acknowledged 'signals':

Eye contact

In order to establish a good rapport with someone you need to meet their gaze for around 70% of the conversation – this shows interest and sincerity.

A nervous person, who makes eye contact for less than 30% of the time, can appear shifty or dishonest. Avoid wearing dark glasses when negotiating because this blocks eye contact and makes you look as if you have something to hide. Prolonged blinking also arouses suspicion. Staring can be interpreted as aggressive. Where you direct your gaze is also important. In a business discussion – imagine there is a triangle between the other person's two eyes and a point above the bridge of the nose. Do not drop your gaze below this. Looking within the triangle between the eyes and the mouth leads to the development of a more social atmosphere.

Head gestures

Holding your head straight is neutral. Tilting your head to one side makes you appear thoughtful and interested. You signal disapproval when your head is down. Putting your hands behind your head demonstrates superiority and a "know it all" attitude.

Hand to face gestures

Our hands can give the game away! Stroking or holding the chin is one of the signs a salesperson looks for, because it means that the customer is considering the proposal and may be coming to a decision. Rubbing your nose or placing your hand over your mouth can indicate that you have something to hide. If the other person does that to you while you are speaking it may mean he thinks you are lying or being deceitful!

Arm and leg barriers

Folding arms and crossing your legs are symbolic of putting up barriers and may indicate a negative or defensive attitude. Clenched fists with crossed arms indicate hostility, but gripping your arms demonstrates a firm attitude. Crossing your arms with your thumbs up indicates superiority.

Observe people's body language at meetings, exhibitions, during presentations and face to face conversations to see if you can interpret what they are communicating.

Strategies to improve non-verbal communication skills

Be wary of changing the way you present yourself in case you appear artificial and insincere. However, it is a good idea to make sure that you adopt open and positive body language if you want people to respond to you. In order to do this try to:

- Relax and smile when you meet people and work in a group.

- Meet people's gaze without turning away too quickly.
- Not cover your face with your hands.
- Get excited and use big gestures.
- Respect people's personal space.
- Resist the temptation to make body contact except to shake hands, unless it is a cultural norm.
- Adopt an alert posture by sitting up straight or standing firmly.
- Resist the temptation to fiddle with a pen or fidget because it is distracting to you and others.
- Practise active listening techniques.

Practise speaking in front of a mirror to see what irritating habits you might have such as flicking your hair back or excessive shaking of your head.

Activity 3.3: Body language

As the Marketing Manager for a fast food chain you have decided to attend a national Food Fair.

Write some notes about the importance of using appropriate body language, when communicating face to face, in preparation for a training session with the staff that you have chosen to represent the company on the exhibition stand.

Planning effective communications

PASS is a useful framework to remember when planning communications. It stands for:

Purpose.	What is the purpose of the communication? What are the main points you wish to get across?
Audience.	Who are they? What do they need to know? How can the message be transmitted to them? When do they need to know?

Structure.	How should the content be organised? How long should the message be?
Style.	How should the message be delivered? What language is appropriate? What format – oral or written?

Figure 3.5: The PASS framework

This Session introduces the concepts of effectiveness in oral and written communications, so use this information when using the PASS tool to plan communications.

Written communications

This section considers the use of emails, letters, memoranda, notices, and reports when communicating with internal and external customers.

Email

Commonly used internally and externally and provides a means of immediate response. The receiver will probably deal with a large number of emails per day so ensure that there is a clear and informative subject heading. It is not necessary to put a salutation (Dear....) but it is polite to write the name of the person you are addressing at the top of the communication.

Internal emails may be fairly informal but must still be accurate in terms of grammar and should not contain sensitive or offensive material. Check the circulation list before sending so you do not send to people who do not require the information. One of the commonest causes of information overload in business today is unwanted mail.

Adding attachments to emails today is straightforward and large files can be sent. However, they will take a long time to up and download so use software to condense them such as WinZip. The advent of broadband communication has significantly improved the speed at which emails travel.

Follow up those that do not receive a reply – do not assume that they arrived, although your mail return system should inform you of this. It is good practice to put a deadline on for any actions you wish the receiver to carry out.

Letter

Examples of letters sent to external customers include service reminders to encourage loyalty, special offers for valued customers to stimulate sales, and answers to complaints. Internally, letters are sent when a personalised and formal communication is required.

Observe the following rules when composing letters:

- Correct spelling of names and accurate use of titles and qualifications.
- Use correct salutation (Dear Fran, Dear Mrs Briggs, Dear Dr. Green etc.).
- Date and give reference if appropriate.
- Do not use technical terms and jargon unless the recipient will understand these.
- Use appropriate tone and approach – polite, informative, persuasive, apologetic to customers who have written to the company with a problem etc.
- Be clear and concise; keep the letter as short as possible.
- Structure the information logically.
- Ensure the recipient understands what response is required.
- CHECK SPELLING AND GRAMMAR.

Letters will usually be written on headed stationery which includes company logo and contact details. If not, make sure these are included. The overall design may depend on the design of the stationery but it is usual to put the name and address of recipient, date and reference on the left-hand side. There is no need to indent paragraphs. If there is a subject heading to be included, put this on the first line of the letter, centred and bold with a space above and below.

An example of a prospecting letter is given in Figure 3.6.

Headed stationery

For the attention of:
Address of recipient

Date

Dear ....

Training to improve performance and results

Further to our telephone conversation, I am writing to enclose some information on the services we offer. These include customised training, business and performance coaching and facilitated workshops.

Our aim is to deliver a product that meets your specific needs and we will work with you to understand your required outcomes prior to delivery. Our Trainers are experienced in this approach and specialists in their fields. Fees for customised training are negotiable so you are assured of receiving great value for money.

As people who have worked in commercial organisations, we understand the importance of developing people in a way that supports and enhances your business. It is essential that new knowledge and skills are transferred to the workplace and so we facilitate this through follow-up and evaluation. For example, all training course delegates prepare action plans to help them continue their development on their return to work.

We are aware that you will receive many mailings from many excellent organisations offering similar services, so we would appreciate an opportunity to come and present our services to you in person. I will telephone you next week to see if this would be useful for you.

Yours sincerely

Figure 3.6: Example of letter

Memorandum

A memo is used to communicate a brief message within an organisation. The information should flow logically and use paragraphs, but it does not require the full structure of a report. If the memo contains a lot of information it may be useful to add headings to the paragraphs.

A typical format is shown in Figure 3.7.

LOGO
Jetsave Airlines

INTERNAL MEMORANDUM

To: T Stag, Marketing Assistant Date: 3 September 200X
Copy: S Ford, Events Manager

From: J Vauxhall, Marketing Manager

Subject: Printed Leaflets for Exhibition 26-31 October 200X

Following our meeting today I confirm that we will require 20,000 full colour, glossy leaflets for the International Holiday Exhibition in London, October 26-31, 200X. We require copy and pictures for the departmental meeting on Friday 10 September at 2pm as this will be the first item on the agenda.

Regarding design, continue with current layout but update destination list and include information on ticket promotions for the next six months. Also resize and reposition the company logo, because this is not prominently displayed in our current material.

Finally, please check arrangements for delivery and storage of the exhibition materials with the Events Manager and report to the departmental meeting on Friday 10 September.

If you have any queries regarding this please contact me on Extension 3345 as soon as possible.

Figure 3.7: Example of a memo

Notices

Notices are used to give a little bit of information to a lot of people – in other words to inform. They vary in size from A4 on a small noticeboard to A3, but are generally not larger unless they are designed for a billboard.

AIDA is a very useful concept to consider when designing a poster because the need to grab attention, stimulate interest, create desire and generate action is central. This can be done in a number of ways – using bold headlines, appropriate use of colour, images, etc. Good design means that there should usually be plenty of white space on the poster so it does not look cluttered and the reader's eye is drawn to the main message.

They are used for many purposes including notices for forthcoming events, general advice and informing of new services. Look at the notices that you see around you – how effective are they at attracting attention and presenting the information?

An example of a notice informing of an event is given in Figure 3.8.

Ready for the CHALLENGE?

Charity Challenge Saturday 10 – Sunday 11 October

Wentworth Outdoor Centre, Wentworth

Open to teams of 5 from all departments of ABD plc, this annual event includes a number of outdoor challenges including fell running and rafting. All equipment provided, teams just need to turn up!

For further information and entry forms contact:

Gina Longman: gina@ABDholdings.com

Figure 3.8: A notice

Report

Reports are written for a number of purposes and range from the annual company report to an executive briefing that would be used to provide the Managing Director with a summary of main issues and potential questions before a shareholder's meeting. Most lengthy formal reports are summarised before being sent out so the messages contained are clear and concise – if more detail is required then recipients may apply for the full version or log on to the company web site.

The Internet has proved a powerful communication tool for companies. Reports can be published on the company web site, thus reducing the cost of distribution.

When writing a report there are a number of questions to consider at the planning stage:

- What are the aims and objectives – the purpose of the report?
- Who is it for – who will be reading it?
- What is the deadline for completion?
- What information is available?
- What research methods should be used?

Reports may be formal or informal (particularly for internal use) but must always be clearly structured so readers can quickly access the information they are particularly interested in, without reading through the full report. Many readers will scan a report before deciding which parts to read in depth. To aid clarity, figures and research findings should be presented in the form of tables, graphs or charts wherever applicable.

A typical formal report structure includes:

- Title page with recipient's and author's names and date.
- Contents page of main sections with page numbers.
- Executive summary – brief overview of aims and objectives, how the report was researched, what was found and what should be done.
- Terms of reference – outline the scope of the report and why it was done.
- Methodology – research design and justification of methods used.
- Introduction – putting the report into context and leading the reader into the main body.

- Main body split into relevant sections.
- Conclusions summarising the main findings.
- Recommendations – what should be done as a result of the findings.
- References for all work that is not original to the author.
- Bibliography.
- Appendices – background information that is useful but too long or complex to be included in the main body.

An informal report might include all or some of the following:

- Report title.
- Terms of reference.
- Introduction.
- Methodology.
- Findings.
- Conclusions.
- Recommendations.
- References.
- Appendices.

In both types of report, all headings and sub-headings should be numbered for easy reference in discussion. For example, if the chapter or section heading is numbered 3 then sub-headings under that chapter or section should be numbered 3.1, 3.2 etc.

Many Managers in organisations produce a number of routine reports and the company will have a set presentation style. This is known as an in-house style. The purpose of such reports is to update other Managers on operations. One-off reports are more likely to be the result of an investigation or feasibility study.

An example of a report is included in the Case Study feedback.

Presenting financial information

When compiling reports and giving presentations it is useful to present numerical and financial information in the form of a graph or chart. All should have a title and the source of data identified.

Examples of the most common formats are shown below:

Pie chart

A very simple chart used to show the relative sizes of factors which make up a total, such as the proportions of total spend on a project. Each segment of the pie represents one factor, so the whole makes a round pie. Once the number of segments exceeds six or seven it can be very difficult to interpret. Also remember to make the colour or shading of each segment significantly different.

The following examples shows the percentage product sales for high street store toy and gift department during December:

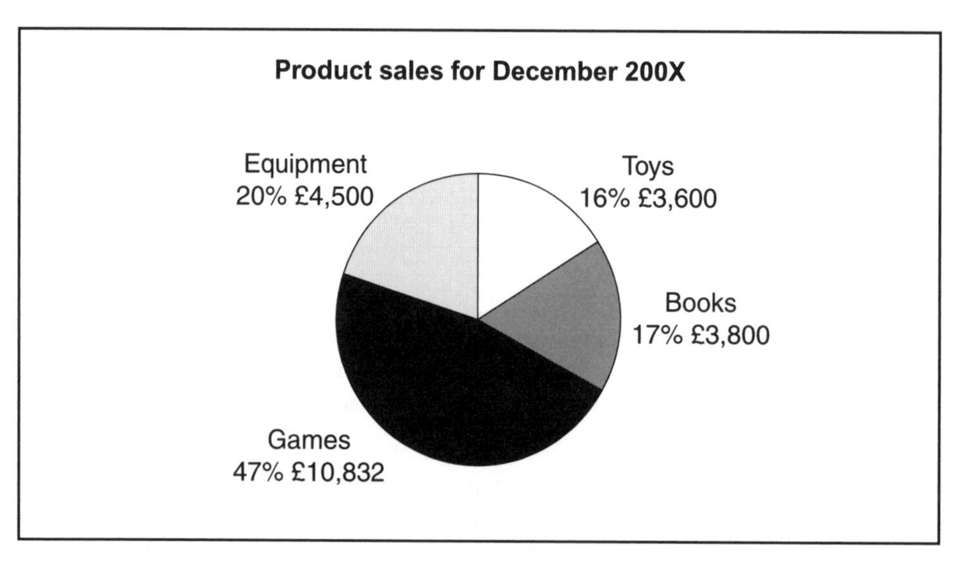

Figure 3.9: Pie chart

Bar/Column chart

A bar chart is used to compare related data and can be represented as vertical or horizontal bars. The bars are shown as separate columns so this type of chart is also referred to as a column chart. Examples are shown below.

The following example shows the use of bar chart to show book sales during the month of October 200X.

Type of Book	No. sold October
Novels	500
Non-fiction	300
Classics	120
Children's	200

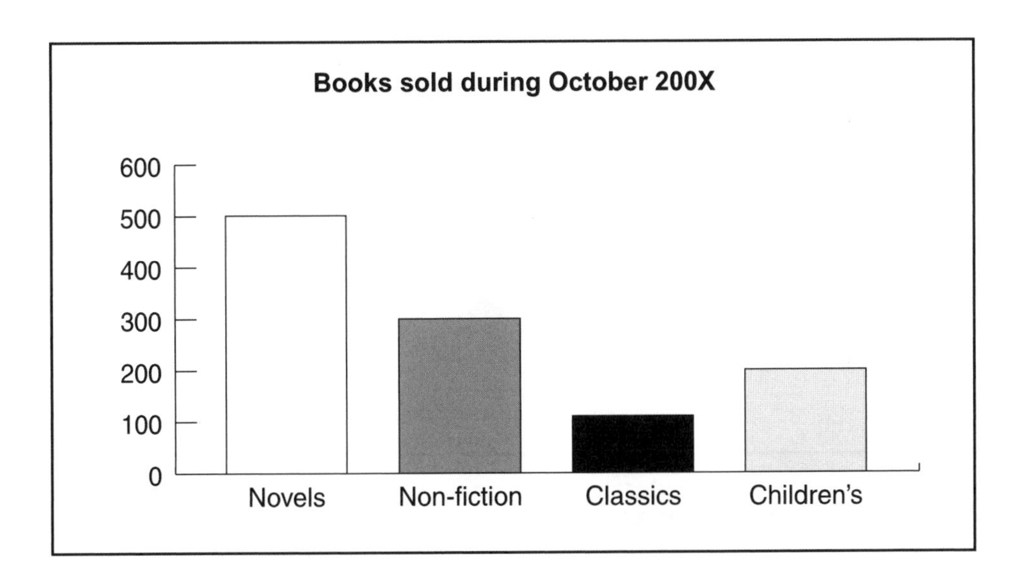

Figure 3.10: Vertical bar chart

If three months' data needed to be shown on the same graph, you would use a different format such as a component (stacked) or multiple bar chart as shown below:

Type of Book	No. sold October	No. sold November	No. sold December
Novels	500	500	1,000
Non-fiction	300	400	800
Classics	120	200	400
Children's	200	400	2,000

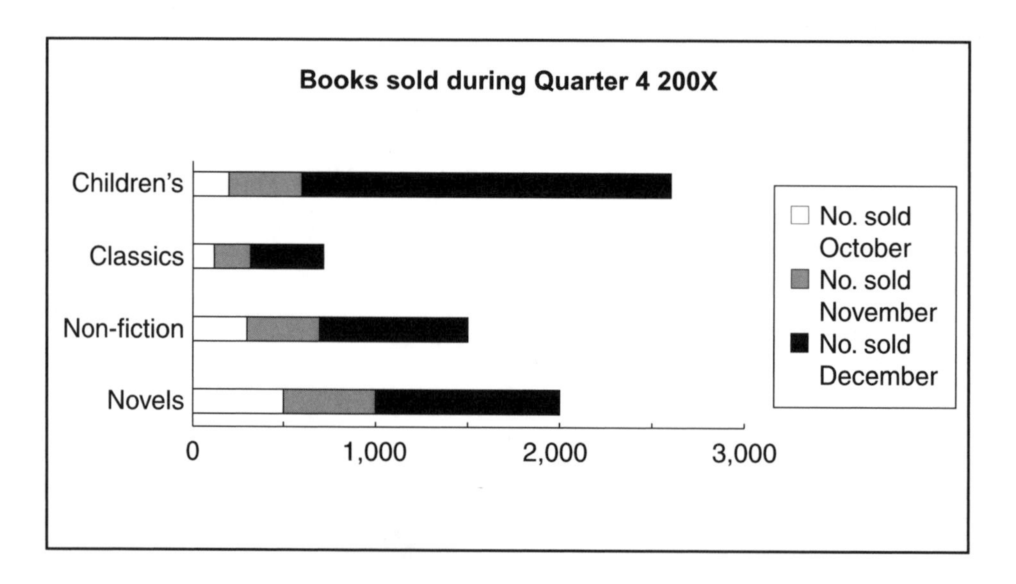

Figure 3.11: Horizontal component bar chart

The above information could also be presented as a multiple bar chart as shown in Figure 3.12.

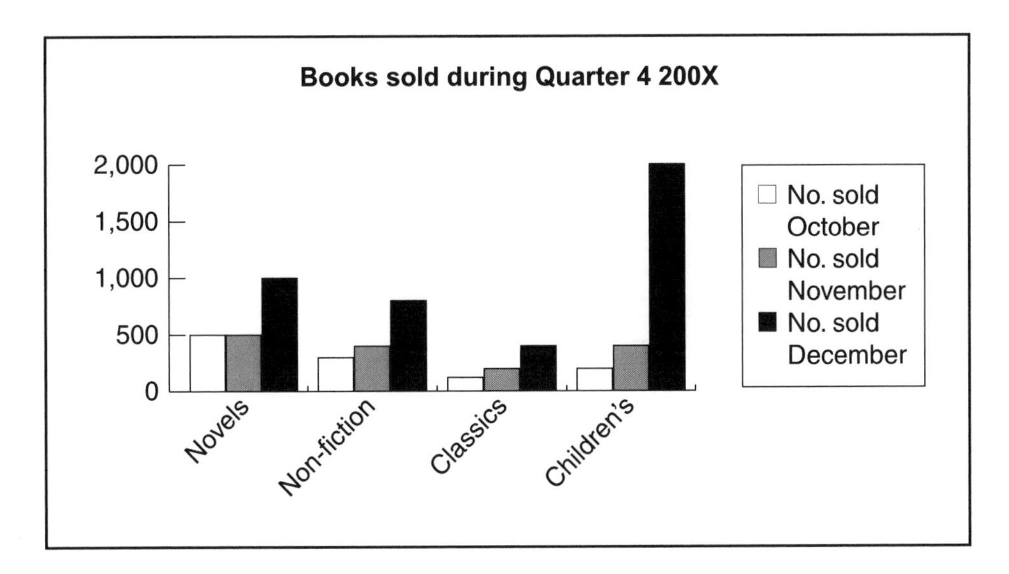

Figure 3.12: Multiple bar chart

Line graph

A line graph is commonly used to show variation over time and is very easy to interpret, as long as the number of lines per graph is limited to three or four. Look at the example in Figure 3.13 which shows the number of bookings taken by a theatre over a three month period for three years.

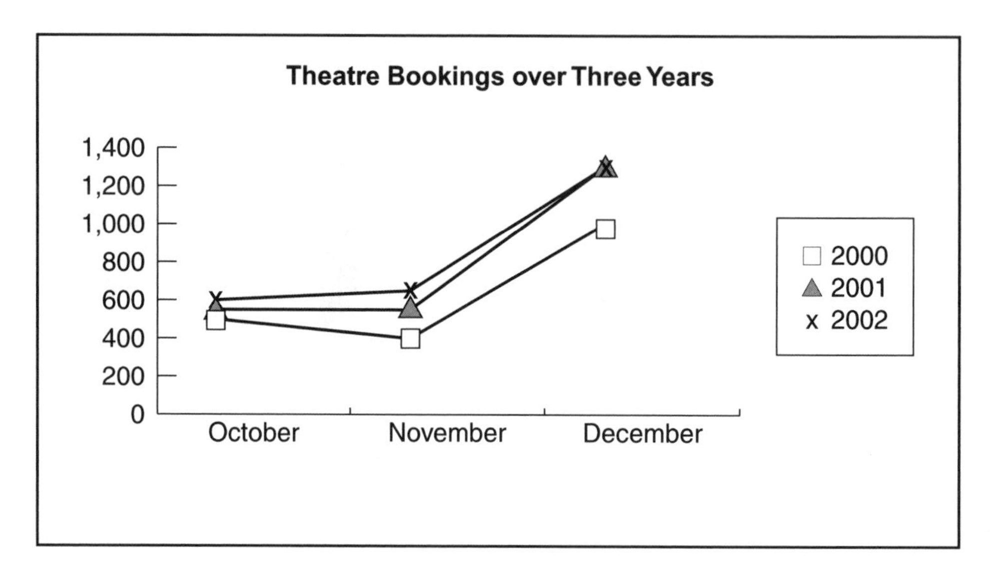

Figure 3.13: Line graph

Summarising and interpreting information

From the section that you have just read on presenting information, you will appreciate that clear and concise reports and presentations present findings in a format that facilitates interpretation. This means grouping like information together and considering the use of table, graph or chart. You will see examples of this throughout this Companion.

When summarising information, select the main topics you wish to cover and summarise the key points under a relevant heading. You may find it useful to use bulleted lists or numbered sub-headings.

To aid interpretation, make sure that the information flows logically and that there are linking sentences used to lead the reader from one section to the next.

You will be able to practise these skills when you complete some of the activities and the Case Study questions in this Companion.

Gantt chart

The other type of chart that you will use is a Gantt chart. It is used by planners to schedule tasks, so lists activities on a vertical scale and time on a horizontal one. The planner needs to gather information about:

- The tasks that must be performed.
- The length of time each will take.
- The order in which they need to happen.
- The relationship between tasks, because some can overlap or take place simultaneously, while others are dependent on the outcome of earlier tasks.

Figure 3.14 illustrates a simple Gantt chart planning the production of a leaflet using in-house design and resources, but with an external printer.

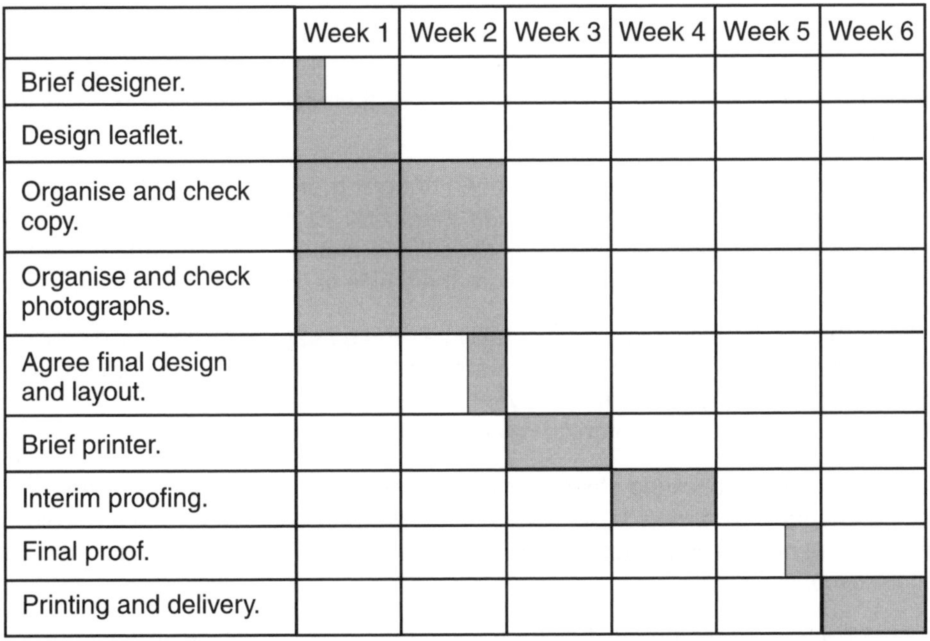

	Week 1	Week 2	Week 3	Week 4	Week 5	Week 6
Brief designer.						
Design leaflet.						
Organise and check copy.						
Organise and check photographs.						
Agree final design and layout.						
Brief printer.						
Interim proofing.						
Final proof.						
Printing and delivery.						

Figure 3.14: Gantt chart

The chart is a simple means of giving everyone an overview of the plan and making sure that people are aware of important deadlines. In the example above, the printer requires 3 weeks to complete tasks so the in-house work is scheduled to be completed before this. Significant changes after the printer has been briefed and begun work may involve additional cost.

Case Study – The UK car industry

Following a much publicised report by the Competition Commission into high car prices in the UK, car makers and importers will no longer have direct control of retail prices. In the past, dealers have been prevented from advertising new cars at any other price other than the official list price. This barrier is being swept away, resulting in greater price competition.

In the past, fleet buyers have been able to negotiate discounts of up to 40%. Now dealers will be able to do the same, provided they buy the cars outright rather than sell stock supplied on 60 days' credit.

Car makers and importers have lost control over supply channels too. Previously, dealers were obliged to buy cars from the manufacturers. Now they can obtain their vehicles from cheaper sources such as their fellow dealers in mainland Europe.

Growing numbers of motorists have been shopping around in mainland Europe. Publications such as *Car Import Guide* magazine have helped overcome fears about the complications involved. It is speculated that unofficial imports are set to rise to 110,000 – which represents more than 10% of the UK retail market.

The growth of the single market mentality has forced car prices down. Any growth in the market has come from low margin business and fleet customers, who account for 57% of sales. Private buyers are staying away from showrooms. Sales to higher margin private motorists have fallen by 6% this year.

Brand loyalty has declined steadily over the past decade and loyalty to traditional sales channels is falling faster. There is a growing realisation that franchised dealers are not the only places to buy new cars and also a realisation that they are more expensive.

One growth sector of the retail motor trade is the new breed of cyber-dealers such as Direct Line's jamjar.com, virgincars.com and oneswoop.com. There may also be more entrants in the form of Sainsbury's and Tesco supermarkets.

Another change to the UK car market has been the growth of the huge car supermarkets, such as Trade Sales and Motorpoint. They tend to promote a friendly, non-pressure approach to selling new and used cars. In a recent survey conducted by *What Car* magazine, they were identified as the cheapest way to buy cars in the UK, offering cars at prices that match or beat prices quoted in the industry's recognised price guide, *Parker's Car Price Guide.*

According to Jean-martin Durst, Global Automotive Director of management and consultancy Cap Gemini, it is predicted that in the next three years dealers will account for 60% of car sales to private motorists. Virtual marketing channels (using the Internet and other technologies) will account for 15%, and independent distributors (like car supermarkets) for 25%.

Source: *Examination paper mini case,* June 2001.

Questions

As Marketing Executive to the Marketing Manager of a car sales supermarket, Jacey Motors, write a brief report on the changes taking place in the car sales industry following the Competition Commission's investigation into high car prices in the UK.

SUMMARY OF KEY POINTS

- Communication is only effective if the receiver is able to correctly interpret the message.
- Barriers to effective communication may be physical, psychological or semantic.
- Oral communication means that complex discussions can take place with speakers using effective communication, questioning and listening skills to gather and disseminate information and check mutual understanding.
- Good telephone technique includes smiling and listening to the caller, so that advice or further information can be provided promptly.
- Plan telephone calls so you remember to cover all the topics in the same call.
- The advantage of face to face communication is that both speaker and receiver can observe body language to help understand each other.
- Memos and emails are ideal for short messages but a letter should be used for a more formal and personalised communication.

- Notices are used to disseminate information to a mass audience so are commonly posted on walls and other like surfaces, where they are easy to see.
- When writing a report consider purpose, introduction, methodology, presentation and analysis of information, conclusions and recommendations.
- When presenting information visually, consider the correct use of tables, charts, graphs and diagrams.
- When interpreting and summarising information, group related points under clear headings and present the information logically, so it flows for the reader.

Improving and developing own learning

The following projects are designed to help you to develop your knowledge and skills further by carrying out some research yourself. Feedback is not provided for this type of learning because there are no 'answers' to be found but you may wish to discuss your findings with colleagues and fellow students.

Project A

Practise your questioning and listening skills to help you communicate more effectively with internal and external customers.

Note the different types of questions you use in different situations.

Project B

Choose a recent situation where you were involved in sorting out a customer (internal or external) problem about which you had very little information, and found some difficulty in communicating effectively with that customer.

Role-play the situation with a partner to bring about a more satisfactory conclusion for you both. A third person may act as an observer and give feedback to you at the close of the interview.

Project C

Read articles in the marketing press that carry financial and numerical information.

Practise summarising and presenting written information by compiling short reports.

Feedback on activities

Activity 3.1: Noise

In the case of a television advertisement, examples of noise include:

- People talking during commercial breaks, perhaps discussing the programme they have been watching.
- Not everyone watches advertisements – they may use the break to make a drink or telephone call.
- Eating and drinking.
- Advertisements compete with each other; after watching five the consumer might remember just one.
- Message is incomplete, hidden or too subtle.
- Poor creative message – does not grab attention from other distractions or interferences.

Activity 3.2: Making contact

The advantages of human contact are:

- Problems can be discussed and solved together.
- The help is there when required; the user does not have to wait for an email.
- User is more likely to complete the transaction.

Activity 3.3: Body language

In face to face communication our body language transmits the real message, so ensure non-verbal communication reflects interest, alertness and sincerity when talking to customers. The following are important:

Eye contact

Engage eye contact but do not stare, as that can appear threatening. Aim for about 70% eye contact during the time you are talking to a customer or visitor to the exhibition stand. (NB. A baseball cap with a large peak is part of the staff uniform. This can prevent effective eye contact if worn so that the peak shades the top half of the face).

Honesty and integrity

Meeting someone's gaze encourages that person to believe in you. If you rub the side of your nose, keep looking away and generally appear uncomfortable you will raise feelings of doubt about what you are saying. Other suspicious behaviour includes rubbing the eyes, looking at people sideways and turning away. It makes the other person think you have something to hide.

Confidence

Demonstrate confidence when communicating by adopting an open, upright posture, meet people's eyes and have your hands held in an authoritative position. Appearing nervous by wringing hands or fidgeting will prevent visitors from coming onto the stand. Other signs that denote lack of confidence include putting a hand over the mouth or lower part of the face when in conversation, jingling money in pockets or passing a pen from hand to hand. General lack of personal confidence may also be interpreted as lack of confidence in our products or company.

Boredom

There can be long periods of inactivity at exhibitions but as company representatives you must never appear bored. Gazing into the distance with a blank stare, doodling or sitting down idly kicking at the floor or swinging a foot sends negative signals. Also, bored people sometimes make audible sounds such as whistling or breathing out deeply, so be aware of this.

Appearing interested

Although there will be many stand visitors it is important that you make each one feel that they are the most important. Use active listening signals such as stroking the chin, tilting the head and nodding to indicate to people that you are thinking about what they are saying. A confident, alert posture will encourage people to respond, especially if you begin to move closer to the stand visitor when they are ready to seek further information, and smile encouragingly.

Product demonstrations

At specific points in the day we will be preparing samples for stand visitors to taste. If you are assisting, make sure that you help the person doing the food preparation by keeping the cooking area tidy and ingredients ready to use. If handing samples round, smile and encourage people to try them.

Session 4

Meetings and presentations

Introduction

Sometimes the popular saying that meetings produce minutes and waste hours is unfortunately true. Despite careful planning and preparation the meeting fails to achieve its objectives, leaving participants frustrated and demotivated. This Session explores the factors that influence effectiveness of communication at meetings.

Marketers also need good face to face communication skills when delivering presentations. The key to delivering good presentations is planning, preparation and practise, so a blueprint for this is outlined in this Session.

LEARNING OUTCOMES

At the end of this Session you will be able to:

- Arrange and convene effective meetings.
- Prepare documentation that helps the meeting achieve its objectives.
- Explain key communication factors to consider in meetings.
- Develop strategies for controlling and conducting effective meetings.
- Write minutes of meetings.
- Plan and prepare presentations that engage the audience.
- Support presentations through the use of appropriate visual aids.
- Discuss how to deliver effective presentations.

Planning meetings

At the planning stage there are a number of key decisions to make and actions to take as outlined below:

Is a meeting really necessary?

People spend a lot of time in meetings that are not relevant to them or that need not have been held at all. Therefore, at the outset establish the purpose of the meeting. Does it cover one or more of the following objectives?

- To gather and impart information.
- To exchange ideas, views and opinions, suggestions.
- To solve problems and make decisions.
- To devise plans.

If a meeting is the best way to achieve your objective(s) go ahead, but always consider alternatives. These include sending a memo, email or conducting a series of telephone calls.

Define the meeting objectives

Ensure that you know what the purpose of the meeting is and what you specifically need to achieve. This will enable you to decide who needs to attend and how long it will take.

At this stage it is still necessary to ask whether the meeting should go ahead. Is a group gathering the best way to achieve the result(s)? For example, can the weekly sales meeting be replaced by a bulletin, followed by one-to-one discussions?

If deciding **not** to meet face to face, always consider the disadvantage of not being able to observe body language.

Identify the content of the meeting

List the topics that need to be covered in order to achieve objectives, and determine the order and how to structure each item. Consider the length of time to be allocated to each topic, depending on how important each is.

Most meeting chairpersons do not pay enough attention to the structure of items. For example, a step by step approach to problem solving encourages people to develop and evaluate alternative solutions. Without this, the meeting can dissolve into a free-for-all with the strongest voice dominating; or no ideas are generated and a solution has to be imposed by the chair; or the item is held over for the next meeting.

Who to invite?

Regular or routine meetings may have a self-determined cast. Otherwise, select people who are:

- Informed about the topics.
- Affected by the issues.
- Able to contribute to the required outcomes.
- Authorised to make decisions or speak for their bosses.

Limit the size of the meeting to a maximum of six to eight people if you can, otherwise you will waste time refereeing disputes or lose focus. Some meetings attract hangers-on who feel isolated if they are not invited. Deal with them firmly but kindly – "Tom, the agenda does not involve your area of work. If anything crops up, I'll let you know" – and do so immediately following the meeting.

Choose an appropriate time and place

The venue must be convenient and have the right facilities and the date and time must be appropriate for those attending. For example, is an early start advisable or do people need time to clear mail? Is a working lunch feasible? Is the lead time sufficient to allow people to prepare for the meeting? Is it advisable to avoid the after-lunch spot? How far have people to travel to the meeting? The date should be far enough in advance for people to prepare their contribution as far as they need to.

Informal and impromptu meetings

Informal meetings tend to be organised casually, possibly by word of mouth. They still benefit from consideration of the above. Select appropriate and comfortable surroundings so people can relax and concentrate on the matter in hand. They are ideal for urgent matters and decisions but objectives must be agreed and decisions recorded so the right people are kept informed of progress or changes.

Impromptu meetings usually happen by chance or are organised on the spur of the moment. There is not much time for planning and preparation so use them to best advantage. If discussion arises that involves others, communicate with them or agree to call a planned meeting. Impromptu meetings work well for small numbers of people who need to discuss issues that affect only themselves. As people are relaxed it is an opportunity to observe body language and receive the real message – which may be different from the words they are saying! Don't forget to record decisions!

Preparing the agenda

Figure 4.1 identifies the steps to take in preparing an effective agenda with an example shown in Figure 4.2.

Agenda dimension	Guidelines
Topics.	■ Be specific, otherwise the meeting will waste time defining them. ■ Limit the number of topics so all can be covered. ■ Allocate responsibility for each item on the agenda to an individual or individuals.
Sequence.	■ Progress from the easy to the difficult. ■ Ensure large topics are structured logically (information, discussion, decision). ■ Arrange topics logically to avoid duplication.
Time.	■ Set a start and finish time for the meeting. ■ Set a time for each item on the agenda according to importance. ■ Consider allowing a break if the meeting will last longer than 60 minutes.
Circulation.	■ Ensure all who will be affected are notified that the meeting is taking place if they are not invited. ■ Send the agenda out a few days before the scheduled date. Too early may mean that intervening developments require you to make changes.

Figure 4.1: Preparing an agenda

The following is an example agenda for a meeting to discuss how to increase sales of advertising space.

NOTICE OF MEETING AND AGENDA

To: K Able, G Bullet, S Cameron, Advertising Executives
From: T Banner, Advertising Manager
Email: tbanner@inter.net

Subject: Meeting to discuss ways of increasing revenue from selling advertising space following the recent meeting (22/6/0X) to discuss the board report on sales figures for last quarter.

The meeting will take place on Monday 7 July from 2pm to 4.30 pm in Meeting Room 4. Please confirm your attendance by email. The meeting is scheduled to last for 3 hours so please clear your diaries for that afternoon.

AGENDA

Minutes of last meeting	TB/5 mins
Matters arising	All/10 mins
Analysis of current advertising income and rates	All/30 mins
Management of key accounts	TB, SC/15 mins
Increasing customer base	Brainstorm/60 mins
Action planning and resourcing	All/20 mins
AOB	All/10mins
Date of next meeting	All

Figure 4.2: An effective agenda

This is obviously an important meeting and one that will debate important strategic issues to make essential decisions for the future. It is broken down into clearly defined sections to aid control and focus. The chair also needs to consider when to schedule breaks and refreshments.

Activity 4.1: Agenda

Consider the agenda below and note good practice. What improvements can you suggest?

To: All Finance Committee members
From: Gerta Holt (PA to MD)
email: gertah@inter.net

Subject: Finance Committee – November Meeting

This month's meeting will take place on Monday 12 November 200X at 10am in Syndicate Room B. Please confirm your attendance by email.

AGENDA

1. Apologies for absence.
2. Minutes of last meeting.
3. Matters arising.
4. Response to internal audit.
5. Capital project – equipment purchase.
6. Update on IT purchases.
7. Sub-committee report on internal audit.
8. AOB.
9. Date of next meeting.

Conducting effective meetings

If you are chairing the meeting, arrive in plenty of time to check everything is ready for a prompt start. Begin the meeting at the time agreed because it:

- Encourages punctuality.
- Shows that you respect other people's busy timetables.
- Is professional and 'business-like'.
- Signals to latecomers that you can manage without them.

Give a warm welcome for newcomers to the group and consider housekeeping arrangements (facilities, health and safety). Once introductions and administrative details have been dealt with, use your opening remarks to set the tone of the meeting. Establish the purpose and then review the agenda. Give a short overview of each topic and what you need to achieve. For example, about the first and last items you might say:

"The first topic is open for discussion – all I want today are your ideas."

"The last item is top priority. We must make a decision on this and allocate responsibilities for actions."

As the chair it is your responsibility to ensure that the meeting achieves objectives and finishes on time. As chair you are also in control of the meeting, so your main responsibilities include:

- Guiding discussion to keep the meeting on schedule.
- Getting people to contribute effectively.
- Maintaining focus and avoiding unhelpful digressions.
- Encouraging diverse points of view.
- Controlling disruptive behaviour.

If not confronted, negative behaviour can prevent objectives being achieved and hinder progress. Disruptive behaviour is due to many causes, including hidden agendas, low morale and lack of understanding. Deal with it firmly and, if things get too heated, call a halt and then reconvene when everyone has had the opportunity to calm down.

When concluding the meeting:

- Summarise important contributions.
- Restate agreed actions and check these are minuted.
- End on a positive, up-beat note where possible.
- Go round the table for final comments if appropriate.
- Schedule the next meeting while everyone is there.
- Announce when minutes will be circulated.

If you are inexperienced, you may also wish to ask for feedback on how effectively you ran the meeting and use this to improve your performance.

Guiding discussion at meetings

As chair you maintain control of the agenda by using appropriate questions and statements during different phases of discussions. Summarise at intervals so everyone is aware of what has been accomplished and what else must be achieved. Figure 4.3 summarises the communication skills and actions that you can take a group through when discussing complex issues and making decisions:

Discussion phase	Possible questions and statements
Defining the problem.	What is the real problem? What are the significant causes? What is the biggest source of trouble? How did it happen?
Gathering information.	What are the facts? Who is involved? What has already been done?
Developing alternatives.	What is required? What do people want? What might work?
Evaluating alternatives.	What are the problems with employing this solution? How does this fit with the organisation's objectives and policies? What resources are available? What is the cost of doing nothing?
Selecting best option.	Which solution will work best? Why is this the best option? Make a decision.

Action planning.	What is the next step? How can this be implemented? What could go wrong? Who needs to be involved?
Reviewing.	Set a review date to check if the right decision was taken.

Figure 4.3: Structuring discussion during meetings

Getting people to contribute effectively

There are many reasons for non-participation including natural shyness, being overawed by rank or perceived specialist knowledge, others' aggressive or dominant behaviour, and laziness.

To draw out the silent and protect them from intimidation:

- Ask questions that tap their expertise.
- Praise their good ideas.
- Openly note their contributions to help them feel more important.
- Refer to their contributions throughout the meeting.
- When going round the table, call on the more junior participants first.

To limit the long-winded:

- Set the ground rules at the start, such as limiting the length of time people talk.
- Request that everyone confines remarks to the topic under discussion.
- If the topic merits further discussion, state that it will be included on a future agenda.
- Tactfully refer to the agenda and insist that the meeting moves on.

To maintain focus on the agenda and what needs to be achieved:

- Summarise progress and remind the group of the required result.
- Interrupt if the discussion is getting out of hand.

- Rescue a confused speaker.
- Call a break.
- Act swiftly when people digress, however senior they may be.
- Be flexible but realistic. Non-agenda items can only be discussed once the meeting has achieved its objectives, otherwise they must be allocated to a future meeting.

Encouraging diverse points of view

Well-run meetings enable a group of people to achieve more than the sum of their individual efforts, through the creation of synergy and the combination of their collective expertise.

As the chair you must encourage all opinions and perspectives to be explored, but be prepared to highlight bias and oversights. Some participants will need to broaden their viewpoints while others must be encouraged to be realistic.

To facilitate diversity and the generation of ideas:

- Use brainstorming.
- Ask open questions.
- Encourage partial ideas.
- Reserve your own views if appropriate.
- Clarify and paraphrase ideas.
- Use verbal and non-verbal reinforcement.

Preparing minutes

Minutes are essential for most meetings. Their function is to:

- Confirm decisions, record agreed actions and responsibilities.
- Prompt action from those attending the meeting.
- Inform and prompt those who did not attend.
- Serve as a record of debate and discussion.

There are two main types of minutes:

Action points, which simply record what actions have been decided upon and who must act, and by when.

Summaries, which record action points but also include a summary of the discussion leading to the action points.

Taking minutes is a skilled job, because the minute taker has to follow what can be confusing and inarticulate debates, and summarise accurately what was said.

The minute taker must be able to:

- Understand enough of the subject to be able to follow the debate.
- Be able to write clearly and concisely, using correct grammar and spelling.
- Identify the speakers.
- Produce the minutes, check accuracy with the chair and circulate the minutes within the required timeframe.

It is good practice to circulate the minutes as soon as possible after the meeting has taken place, so that everyone can be reminded of what actions they agreed to take, and the deadline agreed for completion.

Activity 4.2: Chair's checklist

Imagine that you are chairing your first meeting.

Write yourself a checklist to help remind yourself of the main tasks you need to do before the meeting, at the meeting and after the meeting.

Check your list with fellow students and discuss it with experienced chairs.

Planning and preparing effective presentations

Planning and preparing a presentation can be time consuming and nerve-wracking. It is a good idea to use a checklist, like the one set out below, to help you gather the information you need:

- What is the general purpose of this presentation?

- Why have I been asked to do this – am I the right person?
- Do I need to inform, persuade, influence?
- Who are the audience and what do they need to know?
- How well-informed is the audience already?
- What is 'normal' language for this audience?
- What level of technical language and 'jargonese' will the audience appreciate?
- How long have I got?
- When and where?
- How will the audience be seated – what room layout is best?
- What do I already know about the topic?
- What else do I need to find out about the subject I am presenting?
- What method of delivery is best?
- What visual aids and handouts do I need?
- Do I need to give a demonstration?
- What other support do I, as the presenter, require – music, props etc.?
- How do I need to dress?
- What additional resources do I need?
- Who else will be speaking? What subjects will they be covering?

Generating the objectives of the presentation

In order to do this you must understand the overall purpose. Once this is established then set specific objectives. To help you do this, ask yourself:

- What do I need the audience to know?
- What do I want the audience to feel?
- What do I want the audience to think?
- What do I want the audience to do?

For example, imagine that you have been asked to give a talk on 'The 21st Century Chief Executive' to a group of business leaders from medium to large organisations. The purpose is to provide a general lesson in leadership in today's business environment. The objectives might be:

- What is leadership?
- Characteristics of current business environment.
- Role of the Chief Executive and essential skills.
- Factors influencing effectiveness.
- Where to find further information and inspiration.

The main points you need to cover will also depend on what you need to achieve. Is it your aim to:

- Give an overview – as long as the audience gets the general picture it will do?
- Provide detailed information – the audience must remember certain parts?
- Put forward a point of view – you need to influence as well as inform?
- Propose a course of action – the audience must be clear on what to do?

You may wish to achieve one or more of these but do not attempt too many, or the presentation will be too crowded and may lack focus. Avoid information overload by limiting the number of key issues that you cover.

Presentation introduction and opening

First impressions are very important so find out if you are to be introduced before you start to deliver. If so, then give the person introducing you a script – that way they will recognise who you are and the audience will know what you are going to deliver. It is amazing how many people fail to give accurate introductions – after all it is not particularly important to them but it is essential to you that you get off to the right start.

During the introduction to the presentation you MUST establish your credibility and tell the audience what's in it for them. Put yourself in their shoes. Let them know why they should give you some of their time.

It is also useful during the introduction to explain your approach, how long it will take, what breaks are planned and when you would like questions. The introduction should prepare the audience and the opening provide the impact required to get the presentation off to a good start.

Effective openings include:

- SHORT stories or anecdotes.
- Quotations.
- Relevant or topical facts drawn from your presentation or other sources.
- Direct statements of fact and why it is important to the audience.
- Indirect statements that are of vital interest to the audience and linked to your outcomes – make that link.
- Vivid example to explain why the audience needs to listen to your presentation.

Planning content and structure

When we read a book we retain, and can later retrieve from our memory, information that is relevant to us. If you wish people to remember you and respond to your presentation then you must consider this when planning the content and structure. The content must be interesting, informative and RELEVANT to the key issues. Information must flow logically so people can follow your ideas.

Attention grabbers will be required but do not fall into the trap of raising the level of excitement in the audience if it cannot be sustained at a reasonable level. It is more effective to maintain a steady delivery than put the audience through the ups and downs of a roller coaster ride – unless this is appropriate!

When planning content think about:

- Where you are going – take the audience on the shortest journey from the start to the finish of your presentation.
- Supporting your case with reasons, facts, figures, examples, references etc.
- Using examples that will help the audience apply your ideas to their own situation.
- Delivering benefits so the audience is sold on your ideas, product etc. and want to know more.

Any idea that you want your audience to remember needs to be repeated – in one way or another – from three to ten times. When speaking to a large audience it is very difficult to observe how effectively individuals have understood, so reinforcing key points is important and will not insult intelligence if you do so in different ways.

Closing the presentation

It is important that you close positively but avoid hype and exaggeration – it is much more effective to concentrate on the key issues and reinforce the message that you want to audience to go away with.

You will probably take questions at the end – even if you have been presenting to a small group who have chipped in informally to get answers at relevant points – so you may need to re-summarise, because the questions may have dislodged some of the key issues from the audience's mind!

Ensure that you have a strong close. If you are giving a sales presentation, then re-emphasise benefits. If seeking to inspire or influence, use your personality and enthusiasm. Speak directly to the audience rather than relying on a list of bullet points on screen. This is when you must engage with the audience and ensure that everyone goes away discussing the key issues. Avoid abrupt endings – it unsettles and disrupts thinking patterns.

Prepare the audience for the close if you plan to use a strong image or quotation – otherwise they might not appreciate the significance or humour.

There are various ways of ending your presentation:

- Sum up then state your conclusion.
- Simplify a complex subject.
- Condense your main thought in a witty, colourful sentence or phrase.
- Base your ending on human emotions such as self-esteem, security, the need for a cause or mission.
- Ask for action making it easy for them to do what you want.

Supporting the presentation

Visual aids and other aids are used to:

- Appeal to different senses (acetates, music, demonstrations and sampling).

- Focus attention.
- Create a change of pace.
- Aid understanding.
- Create a more vivid and lasting impression than the speaker alone.
- Reinforce important points.
- Provide reference material for future use (handouts).

There are a number of ways of adding interest to your presentation:

Visual aids – acetates and PowerPoint

A word of warning – avoid stunning graphic displays that reduce your presentation to a simple voice over! A picture can be worth a thousand words BUT make sure it doesn't get in the way of you, the person, delivering the presentation. Keep It Short and Sweet (KISS).

Limit the number of bulleted list slides you use – the audience may be concentrating on one that is more interesting to them than the one you are talking about. Consider using slides that have no words on them at all.

Don't use your PowerPoint slides as prompts for your presentation or you will end up reading them out to the audience and then explaining each point. Very obvious and very boring.

When designing your visual aids limit the number of points per slide – no more than 5. Present figures as graphs and charts where possible.

Guide your audience where to look when you put up a visual aid. For example, "If you look at the largest segment on the pie chart you can see that over 50%..."

Give handouts if the image is complicated so people can see the small detail, if you need to use slides that contain some detail.

Do not turn to read from the screen – you will have lost eye contact and some people may find it difficult to hear what you are saying.

The alternatives to visuals are Case Studies, vivid examples, anecdotes and analogies. Human interest stories are what sell newspapers, so they may be useful for your presentation. Choose material that is appropriate and relevant to your audience, not just because it is the funniest story you have ever heard! Case Studies can be very illuminating but ensure that you have permission to use them.

Using facts and figures

Use relevant facts and figures to back up your arguments and key points but identify the source. Present figures in a table or as a graph or chart for greater clarity and draw people's attention to the specific information that you want them to take away.

Simply presenting a chart that is obvious to you will not work. Talk people through the information. Try to limit the number of segments in a pie chart or bars on a bar chart. Once you get over six it is difficult for people to decipher – particularly if they are sitting some distance away.

Videos

Make sure that you use relevant clips – you will rarely need to show a complete video.

People's attention will wander after a few minutes so prepare them for the viewing by giving them information on what to look out for. For example, "In this short clip of a receptionist taking a telephone order from a client, I want you to look for examples of good and bad practice and we will discuss these afterwards". Check that the video is wound to the right place and that the sound levels are appropriate for the environment BEFORE the presentation.

Product demonstrations

Make sure everyone can see what you are doing at all times and give a commentary on what you are doing or get a colleague to do this. Identify the purpose of the demonstration at the outset and explain what is happening. For example, "If I turn the machine on you will be able to appreciate how quiet it is compared to the current model that you use. In addition, you will be able to see how much easier it is to operate by a single person. This is a major breakthrough, as are the improved safety features which I will also point out during the demonstration." What is obvious to you will not be obvious to those who are not familiar with your product.

Delivering the presentation

When presenting, consider:

- SMILING – it releases a chemical in the brain that promotes a sense of well being and tends to be infectious. But avoid the Cheshire Cat syndrome – don't smile all the time or you will appear artificial. Be natural. Be pleasant.
- Any idiosyncrasies that you have – for example, do you say 'right' or 'obviously' a lot, or shift from foot to foot when speaking?
- Eye contact – do not stare but make sure you include everybody in the audience.
- Standing comfortably but not too relaxed. Do not stand with your feet together because it may encourage you to rock from side to side. Stand firm with your feet slightly apart. Be confident and aware of the way you are communicating non-verbally!!
- How you overcome mistakes – we all make them. Do not apologise, but put it right and carry on confidently. If you are comfortable, the audience will reflect this. If you get flustered or embarrassed, so will they.
- Your appearance – avoid flashy jewellery and clothes that rustle with every movement. Seek the advice of real friends and supportive colleagues if you are not sure what might be appropriate. Check clothes are clean and tidy with no missing buttons or frayed cuffs!
- Wearing comfortable clothes and shoes!
- Your gestures – using your hands can be expressive but waving your arms about is very off-putting.
- Think of the audience as your friends not the enemy – it will affect how you speak to them!

Vocal flexibility

Listen to effective presenters on the television and radio and analyse why you find them interesting or pleasant to listen to. Do they:

- Use their voice expressively by varying tone?
- Vary the pace of delivery?
- Pause after important points and repeat if necessary?

In order to add meaning to what you say, you need to use the right tone and body language. Look at these initially surprising statistics:

When we communicate, the meaning of the message is relayed by:

7% Content.
38% Tone.
55% Body Language.

The receiver interprets the message using the above clues – each of which are open to interpretation and can easily be misunderstood. To stand most chance of getting the right message across, make sure that all three elements are consistent. If you want the audience to be happy then speak in a happy tone and use open body language.

Practice your vocal flexibility. If you do a lot of public speaking, a voice coach can take you through exercises that help you to explore the areas of pitch, rhythm (this involves altering breathing patterns), speed, tone quality (clear, breathy etc.) and volume. Alternatively try the following:

1. Find someone who speaks very differently to you and try to copy their style. You may need to copy their body posture. As you do this try to appreciate how your physiology affects the way you speak. Singers use different postures to project their voices and achieve different notes.

2. Say a simple phrase in different emotional styles, such as angry, sad, happy and bored. Ask a colleague to give you feedback on how easy it is to spot each emotion.

3. Mimic a television presenter as they are speaking!

Controlling a question and answer session

When taking questions:

- Believe that the person asking the question really wants to know the answer – it will make a difference to how you answer!
- LISTEN ACTIVELY and answer what was asked – do not try to take advantage of the questioner to get another point across.
- Seek clarification if you are unsure about what is being asked.
- Repeat the question if you are in front of a large audience.

- Be brief.
- If it is not of universal appeal then give a brief answer and get back to the questioner after the presentation.
- Respond to negatives – refer back to the facts that support your position that you have used in the presentation. Do not assume that the questioner heard these or realised their significance – they may have been distracted!
- If you cannot answer you may be able to ask someone else to take the question or promise to find out and tell the questioner when you will get back to them.
- Deal with non-relevant questions firmly but politely – "if we had more time it would be useful to explore your point, perhaps we can talk further after the event" – do not waste other people's time.

Activity 4.3: The Internet as a promotional tool

As the Marketing Manager of a company selling children's books and toys, you have been asked to talk to a group of marketing students about using the Internet as a promotional tool.

Make some brief notes to help you structure your presentation.

Case Study – Cooper's Edinburgh office

Coopers, a firm of solicitors, has offices in London, Madrid, Dublin and Edinburgh. The Edinburgh office has been open for twelve months and has six staff.

The client list and number of cases per client for the office over the past year has been as follows: PCB Construction (9); Costex (3); NIB Insurance (70); Econ (6); Rosso Wines (5); Perfect Home Builders Construction Company (20); Medcare (2); Commercial Insurance (89); Jenkins & Co (1) and Pemberton & Sons (1).

New cases have come in each month since the office opened in January of last year: 4 in January; 6 in February; 10 in March; 14 in April; 20 in May; 18 in June; 16 in July; 15 in August; 25 in September; 30 in October; 28 in November and 20 in December.

Fees earned by each member of staff at the office for the last year are as follows: Jan Friedland £61K; Richard West £193K; Fran Lee £34K; Alex Fergus £45K; Babs MacKean £32K and Sam Abela £47K.

Sales revenue for the Edinburgh office over the year has amounted to £412,000. Overhead costs for running the office account for 28% of that figure; salaries account for 52% and marketing costs (including the launch) account for 13% of the figure.

Marketing expenditure for the Edinburgh office was allocated during the last year as follows: 9% of the budget on PR; 32% on events; 5% on exhibitions; 47% on advertising and sponsorship and 7% on direct marketing.

Source: Customer Communications examination paper, June 1999.

Questions

As Manager of the Edinburgh office you have been asked to prepare a report of the first year's performance to present at the next meeting of Partners.

Prepare slides to support your presentation on: client list and number of cases per client, the number of new cases coming into the office month by month and fees earned by staff.

SUMMARY OF KEY POINTS

- Meetings are used to gather and disseminate information, solve problems and make decisions.
- Effective meetings achieve their objective in the time stated through the controlling hand of a good chair.
- Accurate minutes should be produced and circulated as soon as possible after the meeting to confirm actions taken and responsibility for undertaking.
- Presentations that engage the audience have well-formed objectives, use strategies to create impact and sustain interest and avoid information overload.

Improving and developing own learning

The following projects are designed to help you to develop your knowledge and skills further by carrying out some research yourself. Feedback is not provided for this type of learning because there are no 'answers' to be found but you may wish to discuss your findings with colleagues and fellow students.

Project A

Ask your Manager if you can chair the next team meeting – or similar – that you attend.

Read through the agenda for the meeting carefully to help you prepare for the meeting and plan how you will manage each item.

If you are not able to do this, use a checklist to evaluate the effectiveness of the chair at the next meeting you attend. In particular:

i) Note how effectively the chair controlled the meeting and encourage relevant contributions.

ii) Note who participated effectively by making relevant and focused contributions that enhanced achievement of the meeting objectives.

Project B

Listen to interviewers you admire on the television and radio.

How do they use their voice in communicating with the person they are interviewing?

If it is on television, observe their body language to see if it conflicts with the words they are using.

Listen to presenters that inspire you to hear how they make use of tone, pitch and pace when delivering a presentation.

What do you think about their appearance?

What impression does that make?

Project C

Evaluate the next three presentations you go to.

How effectively were the objectives met?

How well did the speaker gain the attention of the audience and was that sustained?

What suggestions for improvements can you make?

Feedback on activities

Activity 4.1: Agenda

Main improvements would be:

- Name people attending so other participants know who they are.
- Allocate responsibilities and times to agenda items.
- Identify a finish time.

Activity 4.2: Chair's checklist

The main responsibilities of the chair can be listed as below:

Pre-meeting

- Purpose of meeting – clarifying and informing.
- Setting and distributing agenda.
- Deciding who should attend.
- Arranging convenient place and time.
- Format – type of meeting, refreshments etc.
- Arranging for minutes to be taken.
- Controlling confirmation of attendance and agenda amendments.

At the meeting

- Starting the meeting on time – welcome, opening statement.
- Controlling the agenda.
- Controlling the participants.
- Heading discussions opening out/bringing in/closing down.
- Explaining and summarising each stage.
- Maintaining interest and involvement of participants.
- Overcoming personal agendas and attacks.
- Making sure appropriate decisions are made.
- Getting decisions/actions recorded.
- Closing the meeting and thanks.
- Confirming circulation list for minutes.

After the meeting

- Reviewing and evaluating meeting process and procedures.
- Reviewing and evaluating meeting results.
- Checking minutes prior to circulation.

Activity 4.3: The Internet as a promotional tool

Introduction

- Introduce self, company and credentials as speaker.
- Explain the purpose of the talk and the approach you will take.

Main body

Cover the following topics:

- Promotion and the marketing mix – what is promotion and how does it fit with the other elements of the mix?
- Aims of promotion:
  - To create awareness.
  - To inform.
  - To encourage sampling.

- To encourage people to buy products and services they do not usually purchase.
- To encourage repeat purchase.
- To establish brands.
- To communicate company image.

- Comparison of Internet and traditional media/channels: Identify media characteristics, emphasising difference between Internet and other media. For example, consumers may watch advertisements on television or use the commercial break for other purposes – to make a drink for example. There are a number of other advertisements competing for attention and other noise; and most consumers cannot interact with their TV. The Internet provides a medium that is not real time and is interactive. Customers return because they want information or wish to purchase and can communicate on a one-to-one basis with the company. Benefits for both parties!

- Promotional tools and how they are used on the Internet:
  - Advertising.
  - Sales promotion.
  - PR.
  - Email.

  Give examples of each and ask students to contribute other examples.

- Ask students to consider how a company selling children's books and toys might use the Internet. Hopefully some or all of these might be present in the answers:
  - Online catalogue.
  - Online ordering.
  - Money-off offers.
  - Free gifts with larger purchases.
  - Online club to encourage repeat visits and purchase.
  - Advertising.
  - To inform customers about new products and special promotions.

- The Future – how developments in digital technology will provide more promotional opportunities.

Summary and questions

- Summarise the use of the Internet as a promotional tool, the benefits for own company and potential future developments.

Session 5

Customer care

Introduction

This Session builds on the previous Sessions which have explored customer focus, loyalty, relationship marketing and customer service. It explores the importance of establishing a culture of customer care within the organisation to ensure that external customer care is excellent. It covers dealing effectively with customer complaints and outlines methods for gathering customer feedback.

LEARNING OUTCOMES

At the end of this Session you will be able to:

- Explain the concept of customer care and its importance in consumer, business to business, not-for-profit, public sector and service markets.
- Describe the factors that cause change in customers and the subsequent impact on marketing programmes.
- Explain the importance of quality and customer care and methods of achieving quality.
- Explain the importance of obtaining customer feedback.
- Discuss how to use customer feedback to improve customer care.
- Devise contingencies for dealing with customer complaints.
- Describe how to plan and establish a customer care programme.

Customer care

All companies in all market sectors who care effectively for their customers tend to grow faster than competitors and gain market share significantly faster than those who do not pay attention to this. They are also able to charge more because the customer service component adds value.

Research shows that it costs at least five times as much to gain a new customer than it does to keep an existing one. Add to this the knowledge that, generally, the longer a customer remains with you the higher the average yearly spend, and it is obvious why companies choose to invest in designing and developing effective customer care internally and externally.

Other research by Xerox shows that customers who rated themselves as 'delighted' (7 on a scale of 1 to 7 where 4 was neutral) were 5 times more likely to remain loyal than customers scoring themselves as 6. Turning this the other way round, satisfied customers are 5 times more likely to move to a competitor than the most loyal. This is quite worrying for those organisations whose customers consider themselves 'satisfied' – satisfaction is not enough!

Effective customer care is about delighting the customer by meeting their expectations and then exceeding them. This involves getting to know the customer and continuing to communicate so ongoing satisfaction can be monitored and changing needs anticipated and met. Within organisations, this way of working must be part of the culture, so that internal and external customer needs are met. This was discussed earlier in Session 1.

In organisations, quality management overlaps considerably with customer care in that the company seeks to identify standards that are required to meet customer expectations and puts in systems and procedures to ensure that these are delivered consistently. In other words, that they get it right first time! Quality assurance guarantees consistency of standards. Quality management means managing quality throughout the organisation and continuous improvement means looking for ways to improve what you do for the customer.

Each organisation should have its own definition of customer care that is understood and delivered consistently by everyone at all times. It must be effectively managed within the organisation and measured so it can be improved. Improvements should be what the customer wants, so the data to inform this process should be gathered from customers and staff who deal with customers. The benefits of happy, satisfied customers should be happy staff and greater rewards for all.

Achieving competitive advantage through excellence in customer care means paying attention to detail and looking for continuous improvement in order to stay ahead of competitors. For organisations that don't care there will always be another supplier waiting to pick up their customers.

The importance of customer care in different market sectors

As a consumer you will be aware of the companies that you deal with who consider that customer care is important. It will manifest itself in many ways but overall it means that your experiences with that company are positive and that they make it easy for you to get what you want. In addition, they check that you are satisfied and make you feel that you are important to them. If you do not receive satisfaction you may complain but most consumers vote with their feet and do not return. Think about the organisations that you use regularly – what do they do to look after you?

In a competitive environment it is easy to move to another supplier, so customer care is essential in b2b markets. Company salespeople and Key Account Managers will spend a considerable amount of time and effort in getting to know their most valuable customers well and exploring ways of doing whatever they can for them. This not only means ensuring they get the right product or service but that everything to do with ordering, delivery and after-sales service is perfect.

In both sectors there is often a lot of personal contact so staff need to be well trained in what they do and know how to deal with people in all situations. Organisations operating in the e-commerce market can also be good at customer care but the personal contact is usually missing. However, when things go wrong people like to talk to a human, not a machine, which is a big issue for e-businesses.

Not-for-profit organisations like charities will approach customer care from the internal angle. They do not have the budget to invest heavily in external customer contact but if their staff are happy and well trained then this should impact positively on how they deal with external customers. They have two sets of customers; those that donate and those that receive the services they provide. Gathering feedback is not as high a profile task as in other markets but it is done cost-effectively and relies heavily on internal information from charity workers, volunteers and employees.

Public sector companies are increasingly aware of the importance of customer care internally and externally. Many are now encouraged to approach this in the same way as a commercial business and they use similar tools and processes to do so. Health services and other public services such as the fire service recruit people who are caring, so people feel well looked after when they come into contact with the organisation. They do gather customer feedback to look for ways to continuously improve, but are less likely to send out customer satisfaction surveys as in the b2c markets.

Good customer care is exceptionally important in service organisations as the consumer and service provider are both participants in delivery. In many industries the person delivering the service is the service; for example dentists, opticians, hairdressers, financial advisers. However, they are also supported by other staff who can destroy the customer-supplier relationship if they do not show the same level of care. For example, the receptionist at a dentist must be polite and efficient. If you attend an appointment only to be told by the receptionist that you are double booked you may not be enthusiastic about the next one. If it happens again, you may change dentists, even though you were perfectly satisfied with the care received from the dentist. For service providers, good customer care must be a 'way of life' within the organisation.

Why do companies lose customers?

Your external customers can be individuals or businesses. They choose to buy your product or service for a variety of reasons and hopefully, 'once a customer, always a customer'. Every organisation loses customers but if they are not replaced, the growth of your company is compromised.

Research has been carried out on a number of occasions to identify the reasons why organisations lose customers. Although figures vary, commonly quoted data is that:

- 1% of customers die.
- 3% move away.
- 5% seek alternatives or develop other business relationships.
- 9% begin doing business with the competition.
- 14% are dissatisfied with the product or service.
- 68% are dissatisfied with the treatment they receive.

Source: R F Gerson, *Keeping Customers for Life,* Kogan Page, 1992.

There is nothing that organisations can do about the first 4% but after that they have increasing power over preventing the loss.

An effective customer care programme encourages key organisation personnel to keep in contact with the customer. This dialogue means that new needs can be identified and changing ones accommodated. Competitors will attract your customer's attention so it is better to find ways to develop the relationship. There are many ways that this is done:

- Customer loyalty schemes and incentives.
- Corporate hospitality.

- CRM initiatives such as contacting the customer with details of new products that will benefit them. Banks and building societies have been criticised in the past for not informing customers of new accounts that they could transfer their investments to, in order to gain higher levels of interest. Those that do so may be able to gain competitive advantage.

However, the majority of customers do not return because they become dissatisfied with some aspect of the product service or care they receive from the organisation. Dealing with complaints is dealt with later in this Session.

Planning effective customer care

Many organisations set up customer care programmes to encourage employees to provide excellent service to customers. When planning to create excellence in customer care it is important to:

- Recruit and select people with the right attitude and skills.
- Train and motivate staff to care about the internal and external customer.
- Take care of staff so they feel able to take care of the customer.
- Encourage people to question existing policies and procedures if they feel there are better ways of doing things.
- Recognise and reward good customer service.
- Encourage staff to use their initiative to solve customer problems.
- Empower front-line people to make decisions about how to resolve customer problems.
- Establish clear, concise, observable, measurable and realistic standards of service that people understand how to implement.
- Gather, and act on, customer feedback.
- Involve relevant people in looking for solutions to customer problems and new procedures to improve customer care.

Activity 5.1: Customer care failure

As a Marketing Executive you are working on the development of a new customer care programme.

Your Manager is aware that you are currently studying for a marketing qualification so has asked you to send him a memo outlining the main barriers to effective customer care.

Write this memo.

Quality and customer care

Quality means different things to different people – both a sausage and a steak can be quality products. The focal point is the customer; quality is what the customer thinks it is. If you were buying sausages you would be buying them for a different purpose to a steak. Both products would meet your need in each case – as long as they were 'fit for purpose'.

Quality may be defined as:

- Fully satisfying agreed customer requirements at the lowest internal price.
- Meeting customers' needs.
- Fitness for purpose.
- Conformance to specification.

In a nutshell, quality means giving complete satisfaction – providing the customer with exactly what they want, when they want it, at a price they can afford. It matters because, if customers are disappointed they will go elsewhere with a consequent loss of orders and jobs.

Competitiveness no longer depends simply on low prices. It is increasingly dependent on a whole range of non-price factors, including good design, technical innovation, reliability, on-time delivery and after-sales service – in other words, quality.

A reputation for providing goods and services of high quality and performance that will attract and retain business is the challenge for today's organisations and Managers. Any company can reduce price to increase market share (volume) but that is a high risk strategy. Competitors will quickly follow so the company is back where it started – or worse off, having started a price war.

Concentrating on quality means looking for a greater return on investment (profit) by increasing market share through consistently demonstrating to customers that their needs and expectations can be met – at the right price. It is about companies establishing positive relationships with their customers and leading them to expect more – which only they can provide.

Quality has to be managed – it will not just happen. It must involve everyone in the organisation. In order to provide quality products and services, at each customer/supplier interface the marketer must ask the following questions:

Customers

- Who are my customers? (Internal and external).
- How do I find out what their true requirements are?
- How can I measure my ability to meet their requirements?
- Do I have the necessary capability to meet their requirements? (If not, then what must I change to improve the capability?).
- Do I continually meet their requirements? (If not then what prevents this from happening?).
- How do I monitor changes in their requirements?

Suppliers

- Who are my suppliers?
- What are my true requirements?
- How do I communicate my requirements?
- Do my suppliers have the capability to meet my requirements?
- How do I inform them of changes in my requirements?

Making the complaints process work

Customers who complain are giving you the opportunity to get it right and may return if they feel satisfied with the way their problem is resolved. To ensure good practice:

- Train staff so they are competent and confident when handling complaints.
- Review the complaints procedure at regular intervals to ensure customers are encouraged to tell you when things go wrong.

- Act on the information gathered from the customer so changes are made within the company to prevent the problem happening again.
- Thank the customer for bringing the matter to the organisation's attention. When it is resolved, check again for customer satisfaction.

To deal effectively with complaints it is essential that organisations have a sound procedure such as that outlined below:

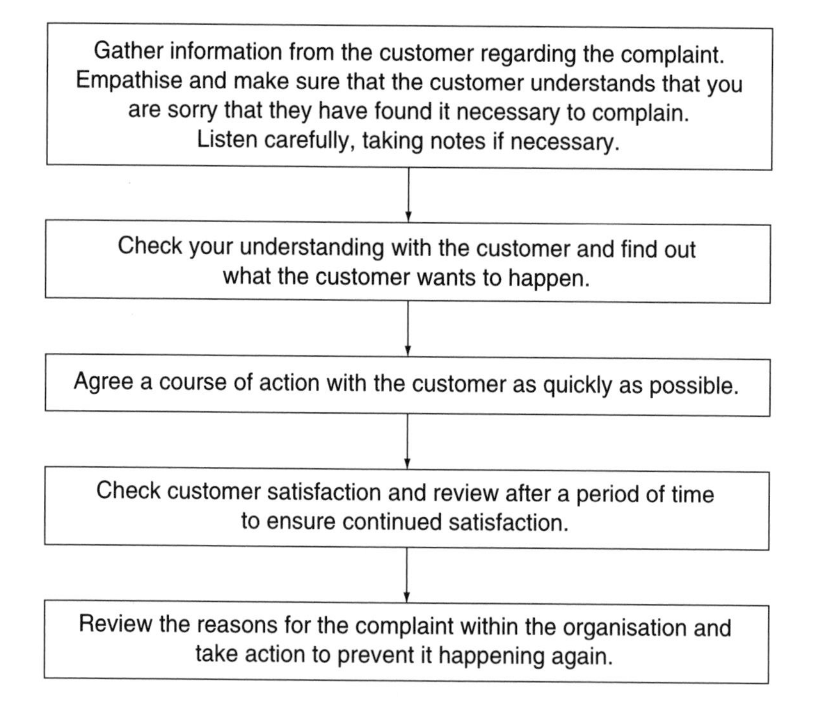

Figure 5.1: A complaints procedure

From the customer's point of view, the fewer people involved the better, because the situation should be resolved more rapidly. Staff who deal with complaints should be confident and competent otherwise complainers will want to see someone in a higher position of authority. If the complaint does have to be passed up, brief the next person thoroughly so the customer does not have to explain the complaint in full again.

Activity 5.2: Moments of truth

Imagine that you, as the Manager, have received the following letter:

For the attention of the Manager.

Dear Sir,

Last week I had the occasion to buy a case of champagne for my daughter's wedding. Your store, where I am a regular visitor, had a sign in the window promising a home delivery service so I rang and asked them to deliver a case. It didn't arrive and when I telephoned to find out where it was, the following conversation took place:

Assistant: 'I'm afraid there has been a misunderstanding – we don't do deliveries of less than half a dozen cases.'

Me: 'Then why did you accept my order for one case?'

A: 'I don't know, it wasn't me that took your order. Whoever it was shouldn't have done'.

M: 'Whether or not he should have done or not, he did, and I've been waiting all morning.'

A: 'All right, as a favour I'll get a case sent round even though we're not supposed to – there's very little profit in our house champagne you know'.

My need, and that of my guests, made me accept your company's 'favour' but I am clearly not a satisfied customer and would be interested to receive your response to this matter.

Questions

What should the Manager do now:

i) To restore goodwill and hopefully secure the customer's continued business?

ii) To prevent the situation arising again?

Check your answers with others to see what different people's reactions would be.

Improving standards

Companies use a variety of different techniques for checking standards of care. These include: the mystery shopper; observation; self-completion questionnaires and reports; interviews; customer satisfaction surveys; focus groups; market research and analysis of customer complaints by type and department. There are pros and cons attached to each one. For example, the mystery shopper provides an insight into staff performance but may also result in mistrust between staff and management. Customer satisfaction surveys are difficult to design and depend on customer co-operation.

Benchmarking is a term used to describe the process of measuring a company's performance against that of another, in order to find and implement best practice. Internal benchmarking compares performance between different parts of the same organisation.

The strategy chosen by the company to investigate their customer care standards should:

- Not alienate staff but raise self-esteem.
- Monitor individual performance.
- Be simple to administer.
- Collect data that can be easily interpreted.
- Set standards for improvement.
- Improve company management of customer care.

Activity 5.3: Plush hotels

As the Customer Services Manager for Plush Hotels you have decided to conduct some research into the customer requirements of business travellers who are regular customers.

Draft an agenda, to be sent out, for a meeting with the Marketing Manager and Training Manager to discuss the uses of surveys and observation to gather information about customer needs.

Case Study – Customer service in decline

The US Customer Satisfaction Index shows that the perceived quality of service across many industries is down.

Although the technology for providing personalised support to customers has improved over the years, customer service, especially online, continues to deteriorate.

In the US, in a recent email response study conducted by the Peppers and Rogers Group only 46% of 65 well known Internet retail companies responded within 24 hours and 20% did not respond at all.

With customers' growing demand both for speed and service, the pressure to handle email quickly and efficiently will increase. The same applies to other forms of online and off-line customer service.

Customers can express their feelings about the quality and performance of e-commerce sites, for example on online rating and opinion services such as thecustomerisalwaysright.com, epinions.com and planetfeedback.com. There appears to be increasing public scrutiny of products, services, suppliers and customer service. Is that the reality?

The jury is still out on how much attention suppliers are paying to customer concerns. The American Customer Satisfaction Index (ACSI), which attempts to measure the perceived quality of service delivery for industries across the US, has found that satisfaction scores for airlines, banks, department stores, fast-food restaurants, hospitals, hotels and telephone companies are all down. Although satisfaction scores are rarely a true indicator of customer loyalty, this is still problematic.

About 80% of the US economy is based on services. It can be argued that slower economic growth and increasing consumer requirement for speed of delivery are contributing to the lower ACSI. But in reality, there are many factors impacting on service perception, quality and value. Perception is the result of the tangibles involved in products and services, such as time, money, consistency, completeness and accuracy, as well as the intangibles, such as reputation, equity and relationship. And these are different, industry to industry.

With airlines for example, performance is hampered by congested airports, staff training levels, food quality, baggage handling, an antiquated air traffic control system, late departures, cancelled flights, and the limited airline choice in many airports. Yet two airlines – Continental and Southwest – consistently score well in the ACSI and both are profitable. They have focused on providing a reliable and strategically differentiated service within the performance constraints described.

Telecommunications is another industry where customer satisfaction has declined. Problems such as billing, directory service, 'slamming' and service outrages are the biggest contributors, and the industry has done little to make changes. In addition, the industry has a competitive strategy of offering short-term user value through various customer incentives, ignoring the longer relationships which customers desire and encouraging switching between competitors.

There are three fundamental issues involved in improving customer service. The first is the attitude of senior management. If companies like airlines see themselves as providers of seats for travel, rather than as service organisations, that shapes the culture, structure, systems and virtually every process within the company. Customer service is viewed within these companies strictly as a cost.

The second issue is that customer service has become more complicated. It may take 15 minutes to sell a long-distance telephone service, but it takes over 200 hours to train a customer service representative. Brokerage firm Charles Schwab, for example, estimates that the length of calls to Schwab has increased by 75% over the past five years. This puts pressure on retaining highly skilled workers.

Finally, the human factor in relationships with customers seems to have been drained from most customer service operations. The technical innovations that are available to customer service operations have only served to remove them further from direct customer involvement.

It may be less expensive to have bank balances available by automated telephone menu, but the empathy involved in answering questions and fixing problems has gone into hiding.

Customer service interaction can be the source of vital information, not just for handling complaints or quality control issues. It can be a method of increasing customer loyalty. Truly customer-centric companies have learned that. Perhaps it's time for companies to go back to the future.

Source: *Marketing Business,* October 2001.

Questions

1. What are the benefits for organisations of measuring levels of customer service?
2. What are the disadvantages of the short-term strategies employed by the telecommunications industry?
3. What evidence can you find in the Case Study to suggest that training in customer service skills is important to the organisation's ability to offer quality service?

SUMMARY OF KEY POINTS

- Good customer care is important to all organisations because dissatisfied customers may not return and may recommend that others do not purchase either.
- Developing a culture of customer care means everyone taking responsibility for satisfying internal and external customers.
- Similar to quality management, good customer care means getting it right for the customer each time.
- Effective customer care programmes include appropriate training for all staff, not only those in the front-line.
- Organisations that achieve excellence in customer care gain competitive advantage and can charge more for their services.
- Organisations need to make it easy for customers to complain and use the information to improve services and customer care.

Improving and developing own learning

The following projects are designed to help you to develop your knowledge and skills further by carrying out some research yourself. Feedback is not provided for this type of learning because there are no 'answers' to be found but you may wish to discuss your findings with colleagues and fellow students.

Project A

Make a list of your customers and their requirements. To help you do so, consider the aspects of your service that are most important to each. Your list may include the following:

- Ease of access.
- Speed of response.
- Same day service.
- Accurate documentation.
- Flexibility.
- Quality of management information.
- Attitude of staff.
- On time delivery.

Are there aspects of your service that do not meet your customer's requirements?

What are the consequences of failure?

Project B

Think about the last time you complained about a product or service and were dissatisfied with the outcome. What happened? Consider:

- How the complaint was handled by each person you came into contact with.
- How seriously the complaint was taken.
- How you were treated.
- Level of satisfaction post-resolution.

How do you think your complaint should have been handled?

Project C

Review the current customer care programmes operated by your organisation, or one you know well.

What improvements can you suggest?

Feedback on activities

Activity 5.1: Customer care failure

Company headed stationery

INTERNAL MEMORANDUM

To: M Harris
Marketing Manager

Date: 4 October 200X

From: S Shearwater
Marketing Executive

Subject: Customer care systems – reasons for failure

Further to our recent discussion, I have carried out some research into the key factors that prevent excellence in customer care and can summarise these as follows:

i) Fundamental to success is the development of the culture of customer care throughout the whole organisation so everyone takes responsibility for delivery. Many organisations have found that delegating the responsibility to a specially created customer service department leads to inefficiency in solving customer problems due to lengthy internal communications. Speed of response and action are critical success factors.

ii) A consistent level of service is important. For example, customers become irritated if they can purchase 24/7 but can only complain between 10am and 4pm Monday to Friday. Using a call centre to overcome this problem can result in the problems outlined in my first point as staff may not have the technical training to understand the customer. Empowering front-line staff is often a better solution.

iii) Lack of teamwork across the organisation causes problems in many areas. For example, customers may be passed from person to person when contacting the organisation for information or to complain.

iv) Failure to analyse and respond to customer feedback is often cited as a reason for failure. Information is collected but not analysed or passed to the right person for action.

v) Inadequate training prevents consistent service. Appropriate training for everyone (front-line and support staff) is essential so customers receive good service at every point of contact with the organisation.

vi) Failure to measure effectiveness means that customer care systems cannot be improved so appropriate measurements need to be devised at the planning stage of the programme.

I hope the above is useful. I am able to expand on all the above points and would be willing to do some further research. At present I attend college every Friday but do not have regular commitments on any other day.

I look forward to discussing this with you further.

Activity 5.2: Moments of truth

i) In order to restore goodwill the Manager could:

- Refund the customer and provide another case free of charge.
- Write a letter of apology telling the customer what action he/she will take.
- Write, but telephone to give a personal apology first.

ii) In order to prevent it happening again the Manager could:

- Talk to the staff concerned on a one-to-one basis.
- Implement appropriate training.
- Make sure staff are not put in positions above their authority.

Activity 5.3: Plush hotels

LOGO
PLUSH HOTELS

To: Greg Jay, Marketing Manager
John Smith, Training Manager

From: Paula Gibson, Customer Services Manager

Meeting to discuss the implementation of research to determine the current and future requirements of business customers

The above meeting will be held in Meeting Room 4 on Monday 23 October at 2.30pm, chaired by Paula Gibson.

Agenda

1. Introduction	PG (10 mins)
2. Current services for business customers	GJ (20 mins)
3. Services offered by competitors	GJ (10 mins)
4. Research methods	All (15 mins)
5. Resources required	All (15 mins)
6. Training issues/requirements	JS (15 mins)
7. Arrangements for research analysis	PG (10 mins)
8. Date of next meeting	All

Please email confirmation of attendance by Friday 6 October.

Paula Gibson

2nd October 200X

Session 6

Buyer behaviour and decision making

Introduction

Buyer behaviour is one of the most fascinating but at the same time most frustrating topics for marketers. What makes a consumer choose one product or brand over another? Customer loyalty schemes are not always successful and competition is strong so consumers are easily tempted elsewhere.

This Session introduces the decision making process that customers use leading up to a purchase. Following a discussion on consumer behaviour and purchasing decisions, this Session explores organisational buying which tends to be a more formal or structured process with key players that the marketer must identify and influence.

Understanding the factors that influence buyer behaviour is a critical success factor in marketing and promoting products and services.

LEARNING OUTCOMES

At the end of this Session you will be able to:

- Explain the importance of understanding buyer behaviour.
- Explain the impact of buyer behaviour on purchasing decisions.
- Discuss the Decision Making Process (DMP) for consumers and organisations.
- Explain the difference between consumer buyer behaviour and organisational buyer behaviour.
- Describe the Decision Making Unit (DMU) and the roles of its constituents.
- Discuss the impact of the DMU and the DMP on the communications mix.

Customer buyer behaviour

It is well known that customers are unpredictable so there are very few ‘rules’ which help marketers to understand why customers make the decision to purchase one product and not another.

Think about the type of purchases you make in the supermarket. Do you always buy exactly the same products? What makes you switch brands and then switch back again? Often we do not go through a logical or conscious decision about what we buy – we do not know what prompts us to do so but we do know that there are many factors that influence that decision.

In organisational markets, although the purchase process may be more structured, it is still unpredictable with many conflicting ideas and needs being thrown into the process from different parts of the organisation.

Imagine that you were tasked with purchasing a new computer system for an organisation. Everyone would want something different and there may be a conflict between what is required and what the budget can afford.

Buying is a process, so there are inputs and outputs – our decisions on what to buy. Because you cannot see the processing that the customer makes when making a purchase decision, researchers refer to it as a 'black box'; the customer's invisible processor.

The following diagram is a simple model of customer behaviour showing inputs and outputs.

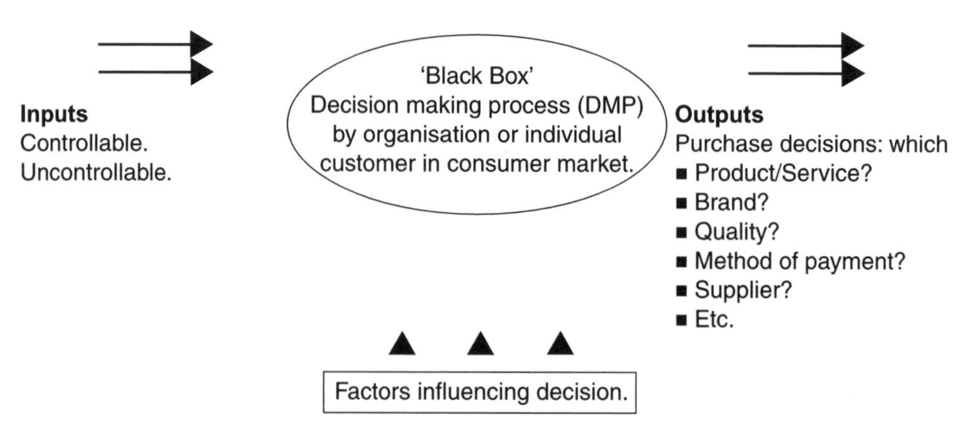

Figure 6.1: 'Black Box' model of customer buying behaviour

The decision making process in consumer and organisational markets will be considered separately, as will the buying influences, as these are also specific to each market. However, the model is similar for both markets. The outputs are decisions on what to buy and that is the result of the decision making process. There will also be controllable and uncontrollable inputs which are discussed in the next section.

In the b2b market the salesperson can often gather feedback from the organisation on why it purchased by asking the person making the purchase. Because the buying process is more complex than in consumer markets there are many opportunities to gather this type of information and other information that indicates why it was chosen over rival products.

In the Fast-Moving Consumer Goods (FMCG) market it is more difficult because information is usually gathered some time after purchase and the consumer may not recall what influenced the decision – or may not want to admit that they fell 'victim' to effective advertising!

Inputs

The decision to purchase is triggered by a set of stimuli or inputs to the process. Some of these, such as price, promotion, product and place (the marketing mix) can be controlled by marketers but others can't.

Consider the following examples:

Marketers can stimulate sales in the FMCG market by incentivising purchase through sales promotions such as two for one, discounts and free gifts.

In the b2b market salespeople can negotiate with buyers to ensure that the purchase package offers better value than their rivals.

Successful marketing means finding out how the controllable inputs affect the output. For example, will making the product available online make it easier, and therefore more likely, that the customer will purchase?

Uncontrollable inputs are the many forces in the environment that impact on individuals and organisations. They are found in the political and legal environment, and the social, economic, technical and ethical environment (collectively, LEPEST).

Consider the following examples:

In a recession, consumers are more likely to save money and cut back on some of the larger purchases they make such as changing the family car or moving house.

In the b2b market, during a recession organisations are less likely to purchase training or do as much advertising.

Activity 6.1: Inputs

What stimuli to purchase might be used by the Marketing Manager of:

i) A charity selling products from less developed countries?

ii) A conference centre during the quiet summer months?

Discuss your answers with fellow students and friends to enlarge your list.

Consumer buying influences

These are many and varied but can be categorised under two main headings:

- Relating to the individual and their personality, motivation, beliefs and values etc.
- Social influences on the individual from the wider groupings he/she belongs to, such as social grouping, culture and family influences.

Figure 6.2 explores these further:

Individual influences	
Personality.	We are all different in our approach to making a buying decision and the personal traits that influence this. Some people are impulsive, some are distracted buyers while others might be extrovert characters who are attracted by a product that appeals to their outgoing nature through advertising or usage.

Motivation.	Individual motivation to buy varies because we all have different needs. Maslow's hierarchy suggests that lower order needs for shelter and security must be fulfilled before social ones, and then those higher needs of self-respect and reaching potential. Some people make purchases that fulfil status needs so buy the latest high fashion or holiday in the best resorts. Others might purchase goods that make them feel more socially acceptable, such as 'energy efficient' or 'green' goods.
Beliefs and values.	Advertising may convince people to bank with the Co-operative bank because they do not do business in countries with a poor human rights record. The value set expressed by the company matches their value set, so influences purchase.
Social influences	
Culture.	The culture that people grow up in influences their values, beliefs, attitudes and behaviour, because they grow up with that history and tradition.
Social class.	Upper, middle, lower, and skilled working are all examples of classes in a structured society. Marketers are aware that people belonging to a certain class have preferences for certain brands, products etc. such as holidays, cars, luxury foods, restaurants, jewellers, and so on.
Family.	The family may act as a reference group – individuals may make decisions that they know key members of the family would approve of. Reference groups are influential groups that the individual interacts with and tends to adopt, or accept their norms of behaviour.

Figure 6.2: Examples of influences on consumers' buying

There are many other factors that influence people such as lifestyle, experience and perception. Like the factors described in Figure 6.2 they will have a different degree of importance for different consumers at different times. For example, consumers may act upon recent experience, such as exposure to advertising when purchasing, or personal circumstances. The first is controllable; the second is an uncontrollable input.

Consumer Decision Making Process (DMP)

In Session 3 you covered the communication strategies used by personal salespeople to inform, influence and persuade consumers to purchase a particular product (AIDA). AIDA is just one of many communications models you will encounter through your marketing career. It is used by marketers to design communications that prompt action by consumers.

Consumers purchase in response to a need – to replace an empty jar of coffee or to buy a more fashionable model of mobile phone, to be like everyone else. The buying process can be broken down into a series of steps during which the consumer gathers information and makes decisions. Marketers need to tailor communications to reach consumers at each stage and to use the appropriate medium or channel to reach them.

As a consumer, you will probably recognise the following steps of the buying process:

Recognition of need – this may be basic such as food, or triggered by wanting to look good by wearing the latest style of trousers, for instance. Advertising often triggers a need or a want because of the way the images are evoked in the advertisement. Lifestyle advertising is used in this way; consumers want to identify with the lifestyle in the advertisement, so are attracted to the product.

Search for information – if the need is simple, such as the purchase of the latest shade of lipstick, the following stages are completed quickly. The consumer gathers information on where the lipstick is sold, what price it is and then moves on to the main purchase decision. However, if purchasing a new washing machine then this stage will take longer. Information on the models available – and their benefits and disadvantages – can be gathered from family, friends or work colleagues, the Internet, consumer magazines, showrooms and personal salespeople and catalogues.

The implication for manufacturers and service providers is to make sure that the information is available and can be readily understood. Branding is important because the product or service is easily recognisable and has a set of followers who will recommend it. The power of the satisfied customer cannot be underestimated. At this stage, recommendation by a person or group whose opinion the consumer values and respects is a very strong influencer. A strong brand image or recommendation by a satisfied client will encourage the consumer to be interested in that product or service.

Evaluation of alternatives – the previous stage often reveals a number of alternatives. For example, a potential customer looking for a holiday abroad will have identified a number of different providers. The task now is to evaluate which best meets needs. This corresponds to the desire stage of the AIDA model. Knowing what creates this desire in your target group is a key task for marketers who need to communicate effectively at this stage. It is important that the consumer is able to differentiate, so it is essential that the Unique Selling Point (USP) and specific benefits are communicated effectively. The travel agent may use brochures, personal selling and advertising to differentiate their product or service from that of their competitors.

Decision to purchase – this corresponds to the action stage of the AIDA model. The consumer makes a decision based on their knowledge of the product or service and how well it meets their need. Sales promotion techniques are often used to encourage purchase at this stage. Direct marketing and personal selling are also useful, depending on the complexity of the decision involved.

Post-purchase – once they have consumed the service or taken delivery of the product, the consumer assesses satisfaction. This is a key stage for marketers because the customer may become dissatisfied at this stage. Organisations have discovered that guarantees or the throwaway line for the salesperson, "Come back to us if there is a problem" do not work. Many customers do not complain – they vote with their feet and do not return. They may also recommend others not to do so either – bad news travels far and fast. Advertising that is seen after purchase may help to remind or reassure the purchaser that they have made the right decision.

Promotional activity impacts on each stage of this decision making process, and a useful way of remembering its role is the DRIP technique.

Promotion is used to:

- Differentiate – your product from that produced by a competitor.
- Remind – customers that they were pleased with a previous purchase of your product or service.
- Inform – potential customers about your product so that they are aware of the benefits it has to offer.
- Persuade – potential customers to buy.

Activity 6.2: The purchase decision

Think about promotional influences on your decision to buy a mobile phone. (If you do not already own one, imagine that you are looking to make a purchase).

Complete the table below against each of the stages in the decision making process:

STAGE	INFLUENCE
Recognition of problem.	
Information search.	
Evaluation of alternatives.	
Purchase decision.	
Post-purchase evaluation.	

Organisational buying influences

As previously mentioned, organisational buying tends to be a more formal and, outwardly at least, a more rational process, and will be described in the final sections of this Session. However, there will be buying influences within the organisation that impact on that decision making process and these may come from individuals or groups that exert pressure or arise due to the prevailing culture or values of the organisation. For example, a strong culture of fairness to all, influences buyers for The Body Shop.

The Decision Making Unit (DMU)

The members of the DMU were mentioned in Session 1 when exploring the different types of customer that the organisation communicates with. In the b2b market, the sales representative will be dealing with a buying centre or unit which includes the following:

Users – the people or groups that will use the product or service so need to have current and accurate information about what it will do for them in terms of meeting their perceived needs.

Buyers – official purchasers who negotiate with suppliers.

Influencers – wide variety of people depending on the nature of the purchase; may also include users. Need to be persuaded by marketing support for the product or service.

Decision makers – responsible for the final selection so the vendor's representative needs to understand the selection criteria they are using, and tailor communications to satisfy these.

Gatekeepers – people who control the flow of information into the organisation and up and down the organisation. If they are not motivated to do this, other people in the buying centre may not receive the right information at the right time. They range from Personal Assistants to Managers at all levels and Company Directors if the purchase decision is to be made at board level.

Personal selling is often used in b2b situations because of the ability to tailor the message to the individuals in the DMU. Organisations are also using Extranets, a password-protected section of their web site, to communicate specific information to key customers.

Organisational Decision Making Process (DMP)

The buying process in b2b markets can be separated into different steps or stages in the same way that it can in b2c markets, but they are different from b2c markets. However, again, each may take time and the stage of the process is readily identifiable, as in the consumer buying process. However, they may take place almost simultaneously if it is a straight re-buy or routine purchase.

Figure 6.3 describes all the different steps in the organisational DMP. The example of a charity looking for an advertising agency is used:

Recognition of problem or need.	A charity recognises that it needs to bring in additional funds and that advertising campaigns have been successful for similar organisations.
Diagnosis or description of need.	The fund-raising Director explores the need with others and identifies the implications for the charity in order to define the specific need.
Product specification.	Exact requirements or specification are drawn up – a creative brief for the advertisement to include objectives and budget.
Search for suppliers.	Potential suppliers are examined. In this case the charity may ask for recommendations from other like-minded organisations, and review suppliers who work in the not-for-profit sector.
Evaluation of suppliers.	Suppliers may submit proposals, tenders or bids according to the procedure laid down by the purchasing organisation. The charity may interview prospective agencies and explore references before drawing up a shortlist. The purchasing organisation should draw up a list of selection criteria to aid the screening process and final selection. All members of the DMU should contribute to this, apart from the gatekeepers.
Selection of supplier.	Proposals etc. are evaluated against selection criteria. The charity would ask the shortlisted agencies to prepare some work to test how well they will be able to work with them, how accurately the agency interprets a brief and how clearly the agency can communicate with the target audience. The decision maker makes the final choice.
Contract.	Terms and conditions and contract for the work agreed. The choice of agency is communicated to the rest of the organisation with the reasons why.
Review.	Work carried out by the supplier should be subject to monitor and review. This information should be available to appropriate people in the future when it is time to renew the contract or make another purchase decision when the same supplier will be on the list.

Figure 6.3: Different steps in the organisation DMP

Many organisations have preferred lists of suppliers for decision makers to use to simplify the process, which can otherwise become too time consuming and inoperable. There is always a balance to be struck between making the right decision in the time available and considering all supplier options; hence the importance of monitoring and review. Suppliers who do not meet specification can be taken off the list.

Activity 6.3

Write notes to the Sales and Marketing Director of a pharmaceutical company explaining ways that a new product can be promoted to chemists and retail outlets.

The chemists and retail outlets are at the 'search and evaluation of suppliers' stage of the buying decision process.

Case Study – Evolving the support chain

When manufacturers start selling new products there are no existing customers. How many cars were there before Ford? Or how many aircraft were there before Boeing? At the start of the product life cycle there is no aftermarket, but today there are 13 cars on the road for every new one sold, and 150 planes already in service for every new unit delivered. This installed base offers a tremendous revenue opportunity, and the manufacturer has an inbuilt advantage. The customer is dependent on the original manufacturer for ongoing maintenance and support to keep the product working over a life cycle of anything from 5 to 35 years.

For the vast majority of manufacturers the aftermarket remains an afterthought, because the business is built around the product rather than profitable opportunities for customer service. However, if we look at profitability it becomes clear that something is wrong with the existing view. Market pressure has seen new equipment margins fall to between 1-15%, whilst aftermarket margins remain a far healthier 30-60%. With the ever-increasing size of the installed base, the traditional dynamic where customer support was a cost of doing business is reversed. Instead of simply being an incentive offered to ease the new sale, the aftermarket has been the hidden driver of corporate profitability. Innovative manufacturers have recognised this shift and adapted their business strategy to survive.

The support chain is a highly complex business, where the performance of the equipment drives both manufacturer profit and operator satisfaction.

7 steps to building the support chain:

- Evaluate the aftermarket for your business – is there a requirement for ongoing support?
- Map the existing processes for customer support and follow-on sales.
- Identify aftermarket competition and market share.
- Identify your unique value (support information, spares, warranty, etc.)
- Leverage this value as the platform for the support chain.
- Apply appropriate technology to improve the process.
- Collaborate with key customers to measure shared cost reductions and revenue gains.

Consider the following example:

GE Aircraft Engines

The $11 billion manufacturing company with a $3 billion aftermarket launched a Customer Web Centre on January 1st 2000, moving one of the most complex industrial support chains on to the web. Within its first year the CWC carried $1 billion in revenue from spare part sales and generated over $50 million in additional revenue from existing customers.

By giving real-time access to over 1 million pages of content – the maintenance manuals, illustrated parts catalogues, and service bulletins that drive customer efficiency – CWC makes GE easier to do business with.

Source: *Marketing Business,* July/August 2001.

Questions

1. What are the advantages that manufacturers are hoping to gain from building a support chain?
2. How can they communicate this to customers?

SUMMARY OF KEY POINTS

- Understanding buyer behaviour helps marketers tailor communications to their target audience to provide information for decision making, influence or persuade.
- The process that purchasers go through when making decisions about what to buy are complex and 'mysterious' so the processor is referred to as a 'black box'!
- There are inputs and outputs to the purchasing process. The outputs are purchase decisions. The inputs are many and varied. Some are under marketers' control, whilst others are uncontrollable factors in the purchaser's environment.
- Buying influences also impact on buyer behaviour and the sources of these may be internal or external to the consumer or organisation.
- The buying process in b2b markets tends to be more formal and complex than in b2c markets and involves a number of people operating as a DMU rather than simply purchaser and seller.

Improving and developing own learning

The following projects are designed to help you to develop your knowledge and skills further by carrying out some research yourself. Feedback is not provided for this type of learning because there are no 'answers' to be found, but you may wish to discuss your findings with colleagues and fellow students.

Project A

Analyse your behaviour when buying different consumer goods.

What motivated you to buy?

Can you identify different influences from different sources?

How effective were marketing communications in the process?

Project B

Within your organisation, or one you know well, discuss how purchases are made and what processes are involved.

Can you suggest any improvements?

Project C

Imagine that you are selling a new catering service to your organisation, or one you know well.

Identify the members of the DMU.

How would you communicate with each one?

Feedback on activities

Activity 6.1: Inputs

The following are stimuli to purchase that might be used by the Marketing Manager of the two organisations.

A charity selling products from less developed countries might include:

- Direct mail catalogues.
- Display material in retail 'charity shop'.
- Web site.
- Email campaign (with permission).

A conference centre during the quiet summer months might include:

- Special offers (sales promotion).
- Targeted direct mail.
- Email campaign to high value customers.

Activity 6.2: The purchase decision

Your answer will probably differ to the one below because, as consumers, we are all slightly different. A decision to purchase a mobile phone might be influenced as follows:

STAGE	INFLUENCE
Recognition of problem.	Peer pressure or situational influence.
Information search.	Internet search of various manufacturers and air time providers.
Evaluation of alternatives.	Word of mouth communication. Point of sale literature and personal selling in retail outlets.
Purchase decision.	Special offers, and personal selling.
Post-purchase evaluation.	Communication from manufacturer – 'club' membership, free ring tones, etc. Follow up emails if permission given.

Activity 6.3

Your notes might include the following points:

Chemists and retail outlets may be aware of us a supplier, but they are not aware of the new product we have available. They therefore fall into two groups:

Existing customers needing information about the product.

- Trade magazines – advertising.
- Direct marketing.
- Personal selling – on routine sales calls.
- Merchandising and point of sale material.

Potential customers needing information about the company and the product.

- Trade magazines – PR – company info.
- Trade magazines – advertising – product info .
- Exhibitions.
- Direct marketing – to previous enquirers.

Session 7

The promotions mix

Introduction

The promotional mix is used by marketers to promote products and services using a number of different tools through a variety of channels. The purpose of the communication varies according to the circumstance, but messages from different sources must be consistent and clear.

This Session and Sessions 8 and 9, examine how marketers use an integrated promotional mix and one or more promotional tools to inform, persuade and influence consumers so they can make well-informed decisions about what to buy and whether to recommend products and services to others. Sessions 10 and 11 review additional promotional activities whereby organisations communicate with stakeholders such as branding, corporate image and exhibitions and displays.

LEARNING OUTCOMES

At the end of this Session you will be able to:

- Explain the role and importance of promotion of marketing.
- Describe the different tools that make up the promotions mix.
- Explain the relationship between the different elements of the promotions mix.
- Explain what is meant by above- and below-the-line promotion.
- Identify how sales promotions can be used to incentivise and influence buying decisions.
- Describe current trends and developments in promotions and their impact on organisations.
- Explain the benefits of face to face selling in promotions.
- Explain the concept of, and need for, an integrated marketing communications approach and the links between communication and marketing planning.

Promotional mix

The promotional mix comprises advertising, sales promotion, sponsorship, PR, direct mail and personal selling. A promotional campaign may include one or all of these tools. When deciding how much of each element to use, the marketer must consider how each activity will impact on the others and how they can be used to support each other. For example, an advertising campaign may support a sales promotion and the front-line salespeople.

When co-ordinating the promotional mix, factors to consider include:

- Campaign objectives – sales promotions and advertising might be used to increase sales, whereas public relations and sponsorship might be used to reinforce brand loyalty.
- Type of customer – for example, as described in the previous Session, in b2b markets personal selling is very important, particularly when products are complex. Many products are customised to meet specific requirements, so the salesperson needs to understand the buyer's needs precisely and ensure that the final product meets these requirements.

  In the consumer market, advertising and sales promotion are more important and likely to be effective in raising sales of coffee, washing powder and numerous other FMCGs. In the not-for-profit sector, charities rely heavily on volunteers and use limited advertising because their budgets are small. Many use telephone promotion to their loyal customer database when raising funds for specific activities. They might also use telephone advertising during a national crisis to inform the public how they can make donations. Public sector organisations are increasingly using advertising to promote their services so consumers are more aware of what is available. Direct mail might be used in exceptional circumstances if a message needs to be communicated individually, such as a change in legislation that directly affects consumers' daily lives. The UK government wrote to eligible households individually offering a grant towards insulation during a campaign to raise awareness of energy conservation.
- Product life cycle stage – advertising is used at the pre-launch and introduction stage to raise awareness and provide information on product benefits, whereas sales promotion might be used to a greater extent than other mix elements during the decline stage to get the last few remaining sales, or during the growth phase to gain market share.

Activity 7.1: Blockbusters

The promotional budget for major films such as *My Beautiful Mind* and *Lord of the Rings* is enormous so activities and communications are many and varied.

Carry out some research amongst your family and friends, the Internet and film magazines into the activities organised to promote so-called blockbuster films.

Promotional activities during the PLC

As products move through their life cycle, different promotional tools are used to communicate with consumers. Figure 7.1 explores the different objectives that marketers need to achieve at each stage.

Stage in the PLC	Promotional tools
Introduction.	Consumers need information because there is no product history to research. Advertising is commonly used to raise awareness together with news releases, PR events and possibly sales promotions, such as introductory offers, to incentivise early adopters to buy. Personal selling is used to raise interest in the b2b market.
Growth.	Sales promotions may be used to increase sales but advertising and PR may keep the product moving up the growth curve. It is important that sales revenues are high, so that the organisation can recoup the investment made during the development phase. The communication objectives are to establish the brand identity and encourage brand preference.

Maturity.	The brand is established, so consumers are well informed, so advertising may be reduced. However, the manufacturer will want this stage to be as long as possible, so may use sales promotion and direct mail to stimulate sales. If the product is popular with relatively few competitors, marketers might consider sponsorship. Customer loyalty is critical to product survival.
Decline.	Once the market becomes saturated, product sales decline and little money will be spent on promotion. Incentives, such as those discussed in the section dealing with sales promotions, might be used to wring the last few sales out of the market.

Figure 7.1: Promotional objectives during the PLC

Above-the-line promotion

This has come to mean mass media advertising in the press, TV, radio, cinema and outdoor. The term originally arose because this was a commissionable exercise in which agencies bought space for the client whom they then billed. It still remains in use for mass media advertising but the fee and commission structure today is not as clear cut, with many organisations negotiating the buying of space themselves rather than using an agency.

Advertising in new mass media such as the Internet is also now considered to be an above-the-line promotional activity.

The use of advertising to communicate is discussed in Session 9.

Below-the-line promotion

This is other promotional activity which used to be fee based activity, such as sales promotion, PR activity, sponsorship and personal selling.

Sales promotions as a communication tool is discussed below, and other below-the-line promotional activities are explored in Sessions 8 and 9.

The change in terminology has arisen because of the new opportunities to communicate and because of changing lifestyles. These changes are referred to as media and audience fragmentation. Organisations need to reach target audiences through many different channels and at a time that is convenient for them, so employ many different tools below-the-line.

Technology has improved the ability of marketers to identify small target groups and communicate specific messages so there has been a huge increase in **direct marketing,** which is now referred to as **through-the-line** activity.

'Pull' and 'push' promotions

Pull and push refer to the way products are pulled or pushed through the distribution chain.

Pull promotions are designed to stimulate consumer demand, thereby pulling the product or service through the chain. Purchase is stimulated through discounts, credit facilities (e.g. a 0% finance offer on a new car), coupons and other means such as advertising. It may be initiated by the manufacturer or the retailer. A manufacturer might direct mail money-off coupons to consumers which can be redeemed at retail outlets stocking the product. Alternatively, a retailer might run a promotion through the loyalty scheme by offering extra points on selected products. In both cases it can be recognised that the manufacturer and retailer need to work together to ensure there are additional products on shelves to meet increased demand.

The opposite happens in a push promotion. The promotion is targeted at intermediaries in the distribution channel to move or push products or services through. For example:

- The company sales force is incentivised through competitions or bonuses to sell more products or specific product ranges. This is usually short term on specific products but in the case of a bonus scheme, may be long term.
- Trade discounts are offered to the retailer if additional stock of a product is purchased, giving opportunity for increased profits. The retailer is then incentivised to 'push' the product to consumers.
- Products offered on a sale or return basis which may encourage retailers to try a new product, or existing customers to buy more.

- Joint promotions are increasingly common whereby the retailer is offered free marketing support such as direct mailshots to customers and point of sale material. This may be further incentivised by the manufacturer offering discounts or additional credit facilities such as sale or return.

Most companies use a combination of both. For example, a sales promotion is advertised to consumers (pull) and incentives provided to retailers such as additional trade discounts and free merchandising/promotional material (push).

Benefits of personal selling

When you studied Session 3 you considered the benefits of face to face communications. Refer back to these to refresh your memory before reading on.

The benefits of personal selling in promotion include:

- Face to face communication between organisation and customer.
- Opportunity to build a relationship with the customer – many buy from the 'salesperson' not the 'organisation'.
- During the selling process the salesperson can help the customer identify needs, find ways to meet those needs, answer customer questions and overcome any objections.
- Opportunity to gather feedback to help improve services and products.

When the customer is searching for information, the salesperson is invaluable.

Sales promotions and advertising are often used to help support personal selling.

Sales promotions

In the retail market, sales promotions are a very common means used by marketers to increase sales in the short term. Setting up the sales promotion means communicating with every link in the chain from manufacturer to customer. More product has to be on the shelves to cope with additional demand, and promotional messages need to be co-ordinated so the customer is informed about the offer and how to access it. It is very easy for one link to break. How often have you seen a sales promotion – for example, a two for the price of one offer on a bottle of wine – only to find that there is no product on the shelves in the supermarket?

The incentives used in sales promotions are becoming much more creative as marketers attempt to grab attention. The benefits offered to consumers include:

- Money-off.
- More for less, or more for the same price.
- Two for one or three for two.
- Free gift or sample.
- Additional points on loyalty cards at supermarkets.

The objective is short-term increase in sales and many consumers will not be tempted away from their favourite brands once the promotion has finished. However, they are likely to use the promotion to try new products, so it is an opportunity for the organisation to communicate with a wider audience.

In the b2b market, sales promotions are not appropriate when products and services are customised, so it is more common for discounts to be negotiated to persuade customers to buy. On large orders for mass-made items, the organisation is likely to be offered an incremental level of discounts – the more items bought, the cheaper the price per unit is. This is to encourage large orders.

Sales promotions designed to stimulate trade sales would include competitions, extended periods of credit, incentives, bulk order discount and free marketing support such as point of sale display material and merchandising.

Sales promotions are not used in the not-for-profit sector, where the main promotional activities are concentrated on awareness raising and disseminating of information. A local college is more likely to advertise its courses in brochures, on posters and in the local press to encourage people to buy. Charities raising money through retail outlets or catalogue sales are the most likely areas to use sales promotions.

Activity 7.2: Getting the price right

Read the following extract from an article that appeared in *Marketing Business,* April 2000, and answer the questions set:

The DTI (Department of Trade and Industry) has issued guidance on price marking in promotions (Price Marking Order 1999). Promotional offers should be unit priced to reflect the single standard product, in case consumers don't want to take advantage of 'three for the price of two' offers, for example. Limited period promotions which relate to individual products (e.g. 100% extra free) may retain the unit price of the product for the period of the offer. This is to stop consumers being misled by a lower unit price in the final days of the offer, when restocking results in standard products joining offer products on the shelves.

Under this legislation, prices must be 'unambiguous, easily identifiable and clearly legible', as must any separate indication of postage, packaging or delivery charges. VAT and all other taxes must be included. Consumers must not have to ask for assistance in order to see prices, so e-commerce sites will have to be easily (and reliably) navigable.

Questions

1. What protection is offered to consumers under this legislation as outlined in the extract?
2. What are the implications for marketers?

Integrated marketing

By now it should be clear that marketing communications and activities are planned to support each other in addition to achieving individual objectives. The overall marketing objectives are developed from the business objectives, so are long term and require strategic plans to ensure marketing and all other functions pull in the same direction.

Operating plans are generated to ensure short-term objectives are met; for example product launches and corporate hospitality. Tactical marketing involves the planning of mailshots and individual sales promotions that are designed to ensure overall objectives of marketing and sales are met.

Organisations communicate with different types of customer in everything that they do. They cannot NOT communicate. Each time a consumer goes to the web site he/she receives written communications. The logo on a package communicates a message, as does a uniform worn by staff, and there are other organisational symbols. If you see a container wagon carrying a product and the brand name is covered in dirt you might consciously or sub-consciously receive a negative perception of that company. However, if you receive a useful 'freebie', your perception is more likely to be positive.

Each marketing activity and communication should be part of a longer-term plan, although the effect might be short term. Each time the organisation communicates with the consumer, that individual has an experience of the organisation or gets involved in some way. These experiences and perceptions contribute to the buying influences described in Session 6.

Activity 7.3: OUBC long-term marketing

Read the following brief extract from an article that appeared in *Marketing Business* in 2001 and answer the questions that follow:

Five years ago the Open University Business Club (OUBC) undertook its first scenario long-range planning exercise. The three groups, into which the 30-strong management team was split, came up with two scenarios – 'Edutainment' and 'The Club'.

The 'Edutainment' scenario identifies a mass market for web-delivered computer-assisted training that would become the province of the giant multinational media corporations. Although this has yet to emerge, we were looking decades ahead.

Meanwhile 'The Club' refers to the traditional relationship business schools enjoy with their students, extended to lifelong affinity group relationships with their alumni. This was the area where OUBC would be best able to develop its business. Amongst the resulting robust strategies were the widening of coverage, which our new MA in marketing is designed to do, and an improvement in services to our alumni to develop the 'Club' relationship. This has happened and we now have probably the most active alumni organisation in the UK. The strategy also called for a richer menu of Continuous Professional Development (CPD) offerings and we are still working towards this. That we haven't achieved the latter indicates how long the timescales may be.

Questions

1. What strategy is the OUBC using to continue to communicate with consumers?
2. Why do you think that the strategy involved increasing the CPD offerings?

Visit the CIM web site www.cim.co.uk to review how the organisation communicates with customers and promotes products.

Case Study – Marketing magic

The Harry Potter series was launched in 1997 with a 500 print run of *Harry Potter and the Philosopher's Stone.* Three years later and three titles later, the initial print run for *Harry Potter and the Goblet of Fire* was 1.5 million copies, 30% of which were sold on the day of publication. Worldwide sales of the series now top 113 million copies, words invented by JK Rowling are in common usage and first editions of her books are sought after.

According to Rosamund de la Hey, Bloomsbury's head of children's sales and marketing, the playground market was important but is always difficult to harness. *Harry Potter and the Philosopher's Stone* won the Smarties Book Prize in 1997, which is judged by children. Word of mouth marketing cannot be underestimated.

The Harry Potter books proved to be a tremendous success story, with distribution spreading quickly from bookshops to supermarkets, service stations and corner shops.

Harry Potter and the Philosopher's Stone was followed by *Harry Potter and the Chamber of Secrets, Harry Potter and the Prisoner of Azkaban* and most recently, *Harry Potter and the Goblet of Fire.* The books have been welcomed by booksellers and the general public for their readability and high standard of writing and storytelling. They have also been credited with revolutionising the reading habits of a nation – Bloomsbury's key brand proposition.

According to de la Hey, the book jacket design was key to creating a brand personality. "The jacket is the shop window, how you create your brand," she says. "We opted for a very distinct artistic style, with Harry Potter in big type and the words of the title in smaller type below. They are instantly recognisable."

"Interestingly, we used three different illustrators, but this hasn't altered the brand perception at all because the blocking is so clear."

Bloomsbury had several competitive advantages to exploit – aside from having won the approval of all key influencers! As a single mother, writing in cafés because she was too poor to afford home heating, there was an excellent publicity angle to the JK Rowling story. The press were quick to pick up on it.

"Compared to most products in the FMCG category, books are able to generate a huge amount of coverage in the press. The Harry Potter series got a huge share from the beginning," says de la Hey.

As the prizes rolled in, Bloomsbury also recognised that a substantial part of the market included adult readers, but that adults were embarrassed to be seen reading a children's book. So a new jacket was designed especially for this market. "It was the same easily recognisable brand with a different take."

Bloomsbury also decided to publish cloth-bound editions for collectors and boxed sets of paperbacks and hardbacks, all of which have proved very popular.

To date, marketing budgets have been allocated to stunts such as a promotional train, publicity tours, in-store merchandising/point of sale and outdoor and press advertising. In 2000, £400,000 was spent on advertising and promotion.

Apart from major press and outdoor advertising, the most successful campaigning has involved "denial marketing". *Harry Potter and the Prisoner of Azkaban* went on sale at precisely 3.45pm on July 8th, a time dreamed up to prevent children playing truant. For *Harry Potter and the Goblet of Fire* the technique was taken still further. A teaser campaign flagged "Harry's Back" and a countdown to publication, but the title of the book was not revealed until a week before publication. "A textbook example of classic PR strategy in action." says de la Hey.

The book went on sale at midnight on July 8th 2000. Queues had started forming hours beforehand and some children had won tickets for special slumber parties inside the bookshops.

To launch the book to the world's press, Bloomsbury hired a steam train, painted it in the colours of The Hogwarts Express (the train from the stories), and stationed it at Kings Cross, London. After the launch it travelled around the country making eight stops and meeting thousands of fans along the way. JK Rowling signed thousands of books and the stunt received coverage all over the world and across the media. The result was 'the fastest selling book in history' (Newsweek).

Source: Extract adapted from *Marketing Business,* November 2001.

Questions

1. What promotional tools have been used by Bloomsbury to market Harry?
2. What unusual events took place?
3. How did Bloomsbury take advantage of the adult market?

SUMMARY OF KEY POINTS

- The promotions mix comprises advertising, sales promotion, personal selling, PR, sponsorship and direct marketing activities.
- Most promotional activities combine elements of the mix in such a way that the final result is greater than the sum of the parts.
- There are many factors that influence the decision of how to combine the mix including promotional objectives, stage in the PLC and budget.
- Different combinations and elements are used in different market sectors.
- Sales promotions are used to increase sales over the period of the promotion whereas other elements have a longer term effect.

Improving and developing own learning

The following projects are designed to help you to develop your knowledge and skills further by carrying out some research yourself. Feedback is not provided for this type of learning because there are no 'answers' to be found, but you may wish to discuss your findings with colleagues and fellow students.

Project A

You work for a charitable organisation that has been established to promote health and safety issues in the workplace. You would like to run a marketing campaign highlighting health and safety in the workplace.

Draw up a plan to show how you would execute the campaign to include main tools used and timescales.

Project B

Compose a poster to be sent to each department promoting health and safety training for staff. What other forms of promotion could be used to support this?

Project C

Re-read the Case Study and make some notes about how you would promote the next Harry Potter book.

Feedback on activities

Activity 7.1: Blockbusters

For the launch of blockbuster films, promotional activities include:

- Print advertising.
- Poster campaign.
- Broadcasting advertising – trailers and previews.

- Media interviews.
- Merchandising.
- Web site with information about the making of the film, the stars and competitions.
- Publicity events such as the opening night with an invited audience of celebrities.
- Sales promotions – these might include competitions to win tickets to a premiere showing, but discounts would not be appropriate and it is unlikely that this type of sales support would be required at this stage in the PLC.
- Sponsorship and direct mail are less likely to be a significant part of the promotional mix for a blockbuster film.

The timing and duration of each would be carefully planned so the effect from one would enhance others – synergy – so that the overall effectiveness is greater than that of the sum of results from each activity. The images used in all media would be consistent, so the brand is established and becomes easily recognisable. One activity, even the most spectacular, would have a limited impact. The integrated approach to communication is much more effective in this and most situations because the message is reinforced via a number of different channels.

Activity 7.2: Getting the price right

1. What protection is offered to consumers under this legislation as outlined in the extract?
   - No 'hidden' charges.
   - Freedom from confusion.
   - Ability to opt out of the offer but be aware of the benefits offered.
2. What are the implications for marketers?
   - Often, promotional offers are printed on the package and may distract from the pricing information, making it difficult to see. This is not allowable.
   - Making the offer price and individual unit price clear while still communicating the benefits of the promotion. This has implications for point of sale material and merchandising – the price message must be as clear as the promotional message.

Activity 7.3: OUBC long-term marketing

1. What strategy is the OUBC using to continue to communicate with consumers?

   - Via membership of the 'Club' – the alumni is a target audience and this type of situation offers numerous opportunities to promote products and services to satisfied customers.
   - The 'Club' demands a longer-term commitment by customers so there is more time to get to know the individual and promote relevant products and services to that individual.

2. Why do you think that the strategy involved increasing the CPD offerings?

   - The message is consistent.
   - It is a relevant extension of the existing product range of qualifications.
   - The target audience has already shown a brand preference by opting to join the 'Club'.

Session 8

Effective public relations and sponsorship

Introduction

This Session explores the use of the promotional tools of public relations and sponsorship from a practical perspective. The role of the marketer working in PR is briefly explored and guidance provided on how to write effective news releases.

In the final section, the reasons for using sponsorship to communicate with stakeholders is discussed and the Case Study examines how PR Managers might handle a crisis situation.

LEARNING OUTCOMES

At the end of this Session you will be able to:

- Describe the role and scope of Public Relations (PR) and its contribution to the promotions mix.
- Describe how PR is used by organisations in different situations to communicate with its publics.
- Explain what is meant by crisis management and the potential effects of PR.
- Understand how to identify PR opportunities.
- Explain how to create effective news releases.
- Discuss how to make sound decisions on sponsorship activities and its role in communicating with publics.

The role of public relations in the marketing mix

The Institute of Public Relations provide a simple definition of PR:

'The deliberate, planned and sustained effort to establish and maintain mutual understanding between an organisation and its publics'.

The organisation's publics are described in the next section. Public relations activities are continuous and are designed either to maximise beneficial publicity or to counteract or minimise the harm done by negative communications. As a planned event they should have measurable objectives so activities can be evaluated and successful ones repeated if appropriate.

PR activities may be organised and undertaken by a dedicated PR Manager or department or, in smaller organisations, by a general marketing practitioner, possibly supported by a PR agency. The range of PR activities includes:

- Open days.
- Corporate hospitality events.
- Special events to mark a product launch.
- Sponsorship of good causes.
- Media conferences.

A variety of methods are used to communicate with the organisation's publics, including:

- Company web site.
- Speeches by key members of the organisation at key events.
- Corporate literature.
- News releases.

Key success factors are:

- Timing of the release of information – this can be critical in a crisis. Delay means that the company loses control of the communication.
- Identifying target audience – some communications will be for mass audience but others need to be carefully targeted.
- Selecting the right medium or media – reach and coverage are important but also 'appropriateness'. Upmarket messages do not look good in downmarket media.
- Setting measurable objectives that help achieve overall marketing objectives.
- Evaluation to learn lessons for the future.

Who are an organisation's publics?

Publics are any group that impact on the organisation and its ability to achieve corporate objectives and satisfy customers. Examples are shown in Figure 8.1.

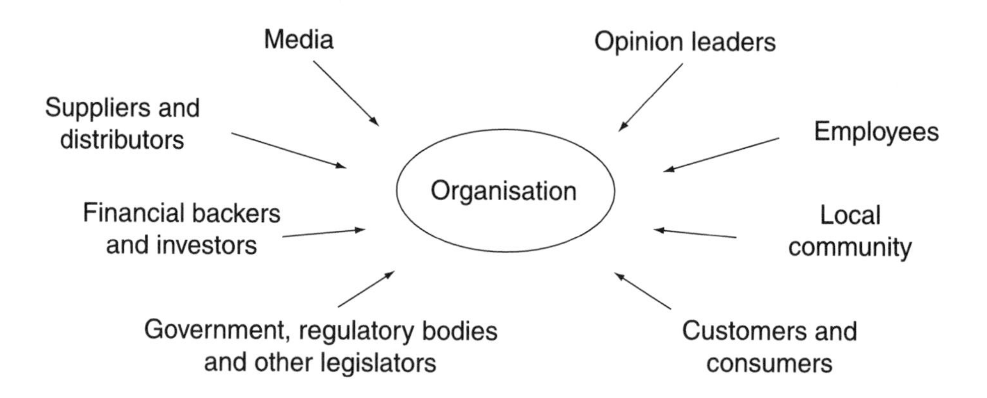

Figure 8.1: The publics in PR

The organisation must find ways of communicating with each of these groups. Messages must be appropriate and consistent. For example, financial backers will be interested in company performance and future business objectives, as will employees, but the way this information is communicated will be different. Formal reports will be the most common means of communicating with the first group, whereas employees would prefer to receive that type of information via in-house newsletters and management briefings, rather than in an indigestible report full of formal language, cash flow, balance sheets and profit and loss summaries.

> **Activity 8.1: Who are they?**
>
> Who are the publics of a football club?
>
> Compare your answer with those of fellow students.

Working in PR

Establishing strong, two-way relationships with key media personnel, and particularly the press, is essential for the marketer working in PR. Often, communications go through the press to the public who may misinterpret or emphasise specific points to make the story more newsworthy.

To establish good working relationships, the marketer needs to understand how to co-operate with the media. The following are important:

- Developing a clear understanding of the media dealt with on a regular basis – readership profiles and circulation details for press and viewer characteristics for broadcasting – so copy is relevant and appropriate.
- Sending well written, accurate and concise, newsworthy news releases.
- Including relevant background information.
- Supplying correctly captioned photographs.
- Co-operating as fully as possible if the media wish to verify facts for themselves, require interviews with key personnel or wish to visit.
- Being a reliable contact, able to provide quotes etc. when called upon.
- Keeping contact information up to date and establishing a regular dialogue to ensure you are informed about forthcoming events such as special features that afford valuable PR opportunities.

The next section explores how to write effective news releases, but first it is important to determine what is meant by newsworthy.

What is newsworthy?

Breaking new ground or being the first to introduce new products and services is highly newsworthy and affords the marketer many opportunities to communicate with customers, publics and other stakeholders. However, it is not often that an organisation has the opportunity to communicate such news.

The editor has to ask himself or herself what the reader will find interesting. It is unlikely to be the same aspects of the 'story' that the company wants to communicate. So it helps to understand what the editor will be looking for. The questions that an editor will use to test newsworthiness include:

- Why is this story worth printing/reporting? What's the interest in it?
- Is it of national interest or local? A national editor will not use something that affects only a local community unless it has wider and more general implications.
- Is it of general or specific interest?
- Are there good images to support the story?

- Is there human interest?
- Is a celebrity or high profile figure affected or involved in the news?
- How recent is it?
- Has it been reported before?

Asking the same questions should help the marketer to send out the right news releases. Bad releases are bad publicity and mean that you, as a PR Executive, might lose credibility. It is also worth noting that news does not have to be new. If it has never been published before it is news, even though it is not recent. However, if other events have overtaken it, then do not release it.

Writing news releases

All releases should be double spaced and have wide margins. Use the following checklist to help you produce good news releases.

- Are the organisation's name, logo and location clearly identified? Local, national and international media will use geographic criteria for assessing newsworthiness.
- Is there a clear headline that indicates overall purpose of story?
- Does the opening paragraph provide a useful summary of the story or news? Media editors receive many news releases every day, so if it doesn't appear newsworthy in the opening section, it will be rejected.
- Is the date to be released clearly shown?
- What is new or different about the information contained within the news release?
- How old is the news? Even if it is not new that day, it is still news if it hasn't been reported before.
- Have usable and attributable quotes from key personnel been included?
- Can the information be used by the media? Is there sufficient background information if a longer feature is appropriate?
- Are contact details provided so further information can be requested or points clarified?

- Is the source of information clearly shown?
- Is the writer's name included?

A journalistic style should be used that is factual rather than sensational. Avoid superlatives. For example, 'This is the biggest and best product that has been launched since…' does not give information. Instead, 'This product has been developed in response to the need for...', or 'the new benefits that it affords to consumers are…'.

> **Activity 8.2: What's new?**
>
> You are a PR Executive at Total PR, an agency that carries out work for Carol Smith, Brand Manager of Webphones. She has asked you to send a news release to the consumer press announcing the launch of the company's new Internet-enabled mobile phone.
>
> Use your imagination to help you write a short press release giving details of the launch date and main product features and benefits.

Using photographs

If possible send an appropriate, professional photograph with a press release, because then the release will have a greater chance of being used. Even if most of the copy is not used, an editor might print an interesting photograph with a clear caption.

At the end of the press release mention that a picture is available but send separately because different people will be looking at the press release and the photograph. The photograph caption should be attached to the photograph.

An editor will not look at a picture if it is not fully captioned, so include:

- Title, that indicates what the picture depicts and, if accompanying a news release, uses the same words.
- Specific information that indicates what the picture shows – names correctly spelt, people's titles, status etc.
- Information that links the picture to the news release so the editor can see how relevant it is – double space text.

- Date – month and year.
- Name, address and contact details of sender.
- Copyright ownership – the editor will assume that it belongs to the sender unless otherwise indicated, so to avoid confusion ensure that the photographer's stamp is not on the back of the photograph.

Secure caption to the photograph so both can be seen at the same time. For example a photograph, 'Presentation of the first prize of £3,000 for the annual Webphones' Team Challenge by HR Director, Steve Price, at the gala dinner held at the Lakeside Country Club, South Wales on 21/05/200X. Members of the winning team, L-R, Tom Banks, Nina Patel, Chris Dalziel.' Plus other details as above.

Identifying PR opportunities

Unfortunately there is no magic formula but using the test for newsworthiness should identify many opportunities. The more obvious include:

- All events and activities.
- Open days and VIP visits.
- Exceptional performance and awards.
- High profile people joining the company.
- Achievements by people of the organisation.
- Crises and bad news.
- Product launches and opening.

Some will have national and international significance whilst others may only be of interest to the local community. Sending the right release through appropriate channels to the people who are best placed to use them enhances your chances of it being used.

Planning a PR campaign

PR is not usually directed at the general public – unless it is a mass media campaign by a public sector organisation. In b2b and b2c markets, it is targeted at carefully selected publics or groups of people with whom the organisation communicates.

At the planning stage, once the objectives are agreed, the PR Manager identifies the target publics and makes a decision on what is the most appropriate approach for each. For example, an organisation launching a new, environmentally friendly product using recycled materials might communicate this to employees via department briefings, posters and notices, company web site and an article in the in-house newsletter. However for other publics, such as investors and consumers, a different approach is required, including news releases and annual report.

Internal PR is as important as external PR. Employees must learn about the news from the source, not the media. This is critically important when there is bad news to communicate.

The results of a PR campaign can be assessed through research, such as surveys, media coverage and response of targeted publics. It can be difficult to identify the exact contribution of each PR activity in integrated marketing programmes which is why it is important at the planning stage to identify how achievement of objectives will be measured. For example, if implementing a community relations initiative, use measures such as media coverage, a reduction in local customer complaints and increased number of job applications.

Press coverage can be measured as the number of times the company name appears, or column centimetre coverage. Readership figures and profiles will give an indication of the number and types of people who had the opportunity to see the message. Television and radio supply audience ratings that provide similar information. In the UK, surveys of television audiences are carried out by BARB, the Broadcaster's Audience Research Board. Radio audience figures are recorded and analysed by RAJAR – Radio Joint Audience Research Ltd. – on behalf of the BBC and commercial stations.

Quantitative results can be measured as above. Qualitative results can be assessed through opinion surveys. For example, is the organisation perceived as a caring organisation following a campaign emphasising social responsibility? Attitude surveys can be carried out internally to assess employee attitudes before and after important campaigns. The way the media portrays the organisation is another useful qualitative assessment – is coverage hostile or positive?

PR Managers use a six point planning framework to help co-ordinate PR campaigns. Figure 8.2 uses the example of a Borough Council implementing a road safety campaign.

Situation.	Following an increase in road traffic accidents involving children, the council wishes to implement a campaign to raise awareness of the importance of road safety among school children of between 4-11 years and their parents.
Aims and objectives.	■ To educate children about road safety rules. ■ To raise awareness among parents and other carers of the importance of teaching road safety to their children. ■ To help Borough primary schools and youth clubs implement an educational road safety campaign. ■ To reduce the number of fatal accidents and injuries to children in the 4-11 years age group by 50% within 2 years.
Publics.	■ Children, parents and carers. ■ School staff and governors, youth club leaders. ■ Local government departments/officials involved in traffic control. ■ Local road safety groups. ■ Road users. ■ Police. ■ Local media – press, TV and radio.
Media and tactics.	■ Information packs for schools including educational activities and competition. ■ Leaflets and stickers aimed at parents and children. ■ Poster campaign for schools, youth clubs, libraries, leisure centres and other public places. ■ Roadshows for schools and clubs. ■ Local radio/television – interviews with people involved in setting up the campaign, news releases about progress. ■ News releases to local press. ■ Press conference to promote launch of programme.

Budget (costs).	■ Printed materials – education packs, leaflets, stickers, posters – all have to be designed and printed. ■ Distribution costs. ■ Promotional expenses – roadshow, press conferences, interviews, news releases. ■ Training teachers and youth club leaders to use educational packs. ■ Staff – internal and agency costs.
Evaluation.	■ Feedback from schools and clubs. ■ Media coverage. ■ Accident statistics.

Figure 8.2: Planning a PR campaign

Use planning tools such as a Gantt chart to ensure deadlines are met.

Activity 8.3: Checklist

Imagine that you are preparing a plan for a PR campaign.

Use Who, What, Where, When, Why and How to create a simple checklist.

For example – the first question on your checklist might be, 'Who am I communicating with?'

PR in a crisis

The Case Study gives some good examples of how PR can be effective in a crisis. Every situation will be different but there are rules to follow that can help marketers and organisations respond swiftly and effectively:

- Act immediately, before anyone else does, so the story is told as you want it to be told!
- Communicate internally and externally.
- Tell the truth and avoid being selective with the truth. Present the full facts of the case in an unemotional manner.

- Make sure the right people are seen – do not leave visible communications to a junior member of staff (If Virgin have to respond to bad news, Richard Branson always appears).
- Reassure by telling people what you are going to do about the crisis.
- Communicate lessons learnt.
- Have a crisis team in place who are trained to co-ordinate such situations.
- Avoid placing blame on others.
- Admit mistakes but explain why it happened and what will be done to prevent it happening in the future.
- Continue to communicate until the crisis has cleared.
- Be aware of the longer-term effects.

Sponsorship

Organisations enter into sponsorship deals to achieve:

- Exposure of corporate name and brand. Large organisations sponsor high profile events and people because of the opportunity to reach television viewers, radio listeners and the press.
- Association of the brand with something that represents the values and personality of that brand.
- Internal employee motivation. Employees are proud to see their company associated with a high profile event or person, particularly if it is a worthy or popular cause or activity. Their success become linked to the organisation.

Before entering into an agreement with another party, important factors that the sponsor must consider include:

- Potential exposure to target audience – opportunity to reach.
- Level of recognition by the target audience.
- Acceptability by the target audience.
- Potential threat to the corporate image or brand – short, medium and long term.

Clearly where there is little opportunity to be 'seen' by the target audience or the activity may contain elements that might be considered controversial or unethical by the target audience, there is no real benefit in sponsorship. It is a difficult element of the promotional mix to evaluate in terms of return on investment, so the best opportunities are those that offer maximum exposure and minimum risk to brand or reputation.

Commonly used in the b2b market and b2c market, sponsorship in the public sector is structured differently. Grants and awards are available for individuals and groups that meet qualification criteria for individual activities such as training or group activities such as the building of a new community sports club. Charities may also sponsor individuals involved in fund-raising activities to help them raise money for the charity.

You will be aware of lots of examples of sponsorship, so start to make a list to appreciate how creatively this promotional tool can be used.

Case Study – Disaster moves

Disaster can strike any company at any time. It can be sudden, such as when P&O's brand new cruise liner Aurora broke down on the second day of its maiden voyage. Or it can be a slow-burn situation that has the potential to escalate.

Prompt action saved the day for P&O. Passengers were immediately told that they would get a full refund and a free cruise of the same value. As the ship limped back to Southampton there was a party on board with free drinks. As a result, most passengers when interviewed by the media were sympathetic and philosophical. What could have been a public relations calamity was averted.

Coca-Cola was accused of being slow to react when, in 1999, contamination in the production chain was held to be the cause of sickness, stomach aches and dizziness in Belgium and northern France. The sale of Coca-Cola products was banned in Belgium, Luxembourg and parts of the Middle East. Sales of canned Coke were also halted in France, and in the Netherlands, Belgian imports were destroyed.

Coca-Cola could have retrieved the situation earlier had it not hesitated on the recall. Its head office in Atlanta was apparently unaware of the Belgian government's sensitivity to food scares, having itself recently been heavily criticised over its handling of an issue of tainted poultry and eggs. So the government took the initiative away from Coca-Cola by instituting the ban. Since then the company has appointed a CEO for Europe with greater powers over local strategies.

This had echoes of Perrier's catastrophe 10 years previously, when a massive recall was triggered by the US Food & Drink Administration, not the company. Share value plunged, and this led to the company's subsequent takeover by the Nestlé group.

Transport calamities can cause unease about whole industries and not just the company directly concerned. Airlines and train companies usually suspend advertising when there has been a serious accident, even if they have not been involved. This is out of respect for the feelings of those affected and for the commercial reason of not wanting their brand to be linked in the public mind with reports of the event.

The Paddington rail disaster (London UK) was particularly horrific. Railtrack, Great Western and Thames Trains put crisis management procedures into immediate effect to respond to demand for information from the media and public, and to express sympathy for the bereaved and injured. However, they did their images no good by appearing at times to be attempting to shift blame from one to the other.

"Tell it all, tell it fast and tell it truthfully," is the advice of Michael Regester, whose company Regester Larkin specialises in the strategic management of risk. "If you don't tell it yourself there are plenty of people out there who will tell it for you. They won't be as clued up with what has happened and may be maliciously inclined towards you or have a different agenda."

The costs of disasters are not just the immediate ones. Often the greater cost and one more difficult to recuperate is the loss of market share through damage to reputation. Share prices may suffer, leading to calls for heads to roll in the boardroom or leaving the company vulnerable to takeover.

All stakeholders need to be considered in crisis management – customers, shareholders and staff. "The key is to acknowledge the genuine concerns of people over things that have happened or are perceived to be happening," Regester says. "For example, staff should not be left to learn about a situation in the media."

A flood of journalists on the phone or doorstep needs to be managed at a senior level. The media won't wait for a press conference later in the day. An early, initial statement is required.

Source: Extract from article that appeared in *Marketing Business,* June 2000.

Questions

1. What was the difference in the response to crises by P&O and Coca-Cola in the Case Study?
2. What were the results?
3. What are the potential costs of crisis?
4. Why is it good advice to tell it all and tell it quick?

SUMMARY OF KEY POINTS

- PR and sponsorship are elements of the mix that can provide long-term benefits for the organisation.
- PR may be planned to take advantage of opportunity to communicate, or unplanned when disaster strikes.
- Campaigns must be carefully planned so objectives are measurable and in line with overall marketing objectives.
- In a crisis, communication must be swift and truthful.
- Sponsorship offers organisations opportunities to reach large numbers of people whom they would not otherwise communicate with.
- Sponsorship is used widely in b2b, b2c and not-for-profit sectors of the market.

Improving and developing own learning

The following projects are designed to help you to develop your knowledge and skills further by carrying out some research yourself. Feedback is not provided for this type of learning because there are no 'answers' to be found, but you may wish to discuss your findings with colleagues and fellow students.

Project A

Reflect on recent events within your organisation, or one you know well. How newsworthy were they?

Were news releases sent to relevant editors?

How were they used by the media?

Consider what is happening now – what is potentially newsworthy?

Project B

For a product that you know well, imagine that it is just about to be launched.

Write an appropriate press release and decide which newspapers, magazines and/or journals it should be sent to.

Project C

Reflect on the different sponsorship activities that you are aware of within your industry and locality.

What is being sponsored?

Can you find some more unusual examples, such as a road traffic island or hot air balloon race?

Why do you think the sponsors felt it was appropriate to link their brand to that particular activity or object?

Feedback on activities

Activity 8.1: Who are they?

Like all businesses, football clubs understand the importance of communicating with their publics and develop marketing programmes and events to satisfy this need. The publics of a football club include:

- Supporters, customers and other 'users'.
- Local community – from whom they will draw potential employees. Also current employees and residents who live near the ground.
- Police and other emergency services.
- Consumer and pressure groups.
- The media – local, national and international.
- Suppliers.
- Distributors.
- Industry regulators and professional bodies.
- Sports bodies.
- Financial bodies.
- Government bodies.
- Players and other employees.
- Other clubs they interact with.

Activity 8.2: What's new?

The press release should be written on corporate notepaper and in clear, journalistic style to include a brief, descriptive heading, main news points and relevant quote. Editors also require some background information about the company and development of the product. Do not forget contact details, in case they wish to do a full feature or check information.

The release would be double spaced with wide margins.

LOGO

News from WEBPHONEs

23 October 200X

Launch of first user-friendly Internet-enabled mobile phone – WebOne – November 200X.

November sees the introduction of WebOne, the Internet-enabled mobile phone, to Webphone's 33 retail outlets throughout Europe and Asia. Competitively priced, it is the first of its type to recognise that many consumers are not at home with new technology so all services are very easy to use.

Users will be able to use WebOne to send emails, browse the Internet, check their share prices, play games and much more. For the first time, users will also be able to bank online and the ability to carry out more personal transactions will be available in six months' time.

Recent research, conducted by Comex, indicates that more than 40% of current users of Internet-enabled phones want to upgrade within 2 years because of the increased screen sizes which are now becoming available. WebOne's screen will be significantly larger than current products with enhanced resolution.

Webphones R&D Director, Sidney Webster is confident that consumers will want this product because of its attractive price, enhanced features and ease of use, "For the first time we have been able to produce a sophisticated product that consumers will be able to use within minutes of purchase – all features are exceptionally easy to access – we know this product is an absolute winner and a real challenge for our competitors."

Ends

Notes to Editors

Webphones was established in 1991 and has consistently produced products that have become market leaders within 6 months of launch. They have a reputation for listening to customers and employing the latest technology to create products that are ahead of their time. Owned by TEL plc, share prices were at an all time high in anticipation of the launch announcement.

Further information from Carol Smith, Brand Manager, Webphones
Issued by P Ross, Total PR, London, Tel: 0171 123654

Page 1 of 1

Webphones, 3 Lyon Street, London SW10, Tel: 0171 333444, Fax 0171 555666

Activity 8.3: Checklist

Your list will probably include some or all of the following questions:

- Who am I communicating with?
- Why?
- What do I need to communicate?
- When do I need to do it?
- Where do I need to do it?
- How much can I spend?
- What tools and techniques should I use?
- What resources are available?
- How can I evaluate effectiveness?
- What are the barriers to success?

Session 9

Advertising and direct mail

Introduction

This Session explores the role of advertising in the marketing mix and discusses the factors that influence effectiveness. We will also briefly examine the different stages of advertising campaigns from conception to implementation. The second part of this Session moves onto direct mail and looks at different forms of mail and how this is changing.

LEARNING OUTCOMES

At the end of this Session you will be able to:

- Discuss how organisations use advertising to communicate.
- Explain the part that advertising plays in the promotions mix.
- Explain the key stages and considerations when developing and designing advertising.
- Distinguish between the different forms of integrated mail media such as direct mail leaflets and mail order advertising.

The role of advertising in the marketing mix

Advertising is one element of the promotional mix and is more effective if used as part of an integrated campaign, so consumers see and hear the same message via a number of different channels. Effective marketing combines the different tools of the promotional mix in ways that the effect of one element enhances the effect of another.

Advertising is commonly used to support a sales promotion and personal selling. For example, as a consumer you may see a television advertisement about a new type of stereo, so you go to a store that sells electric goods and talk to a salesperson about its features and benefits. Advertising is used to 'pull' the product through the distribution channels.

Uses of advertising

Some of the major uses for advertising are:

- To stimulate demand, as in the above example.
- To create awareness or inform the market – commonly used during the early stages of the PLC.
- To educate – the not-for-profit sectors might promote public services this way using mass media campaigns. Political organisations use extensive poster campaigns during general elections in the UK.
- To remind and reinforce – used at later stages of the PLC when consumers are well informed, or in b2b markets to keep the company or brand high profile.
- To influence or persuade consumers to develop brand preference.
- To counter competitors' advertising to highlight the different features and benefits of your brand over rival products.

Different types of advertising

Mass media advertising is commonly referred to as above-the-line promotional activity and includes:

Television advertising

Many people spend some part of every day watching television and new channels are becoming available continuously. Viewer profiles are available so marketers can target more accurately, especially as some channels cater for specific interests, geographic locations or age groups.

As a creative medium, impact can be created via sound, vision and movement, so advertisers are becoming very sophisticated in the storylines they introduce. The main disadvantage is cost and competition. Your advertisement may be one of several 30 second slots that viewers see during a commercial break – that is if they are not changing channels or getting up to make a drink!

Radio advertising

Relying as it does on sound, radio advertising is not as creative a medium as television but can use famous voices to add interest and association. The voice used for the advertisement is obviously critical for success so qualities such as pitch and tone are as important as pace in delivery of the message.

Radio stations cater for different audiences so marketers can use this information to help target specific groups. The advantage of radio advertising is that it is much cheaper than television, and recent research indicates that its effectiveness is higher too. This is largely because people continue listening to the radio whatever they are doing, and so absorb the advertising; they do not change channels or leave the room when the advertising is on, or they are listening to the radio in the car, and thus are a more captive audience than when they are watching television.

Cinema advertising

Cinema offers opportunities to create impact through the use of sound, movement, visual effects and size of screen. It is used to promote forthcoming attractions by offering a 'taster' through showing action clips that introduce the characters and story. The medium can be used to better effect than television advertising because the audience is less likely to get up and make a cup of tea and cannot switch channels! They are more likely to be watching the screen. The main downside is cost, which is even higher than television.

Outdoor/Poster advertising

Posters are a much more limited medium than broadcast media. Exposure time is brief so the message must be short. Strong colours and bold images can be used to create impact but there is usually no opportunity for sound and movement. Posters are useful because large numbers of people will see them and, if they go past frequently, will see the same image over and over again. They can be used outdoors and indoors and on moving sites such as buses, taxis and tube trains.

Other types of outdoor advertising include banners streamed from planes or on poles. Look around for as many examples as you can.

Press advertising

This refers to all printed media so includes newspapers, journals and magazines, giving the marketer an enormous choice. However, different media cater for specific groups. Some of these are quite small and advertising rates reflect this. Advertising in local press is much less expensive than national newspapers.

The advantage of the printed media for b2b markets and not-for-profit sectors is that many trade journals are highly specific and circulated through subscription to a high number of the target audience.

As a medium it offers many opportunities to create visual impact but is not dynamic. Different positions in the printed media will be more expensive as these are those most likely to be seen by readers. Front and back covers normally attract a premium. A further advantage is that editors may offer the opportunity to do an 'advertorial'. This is where a feature is run on the subject in collaboration with the advertiser, and includes advertising elements of the product or service, with details of how the product or service can be purchased. The benefit of this is that people are more likely to read it because it is presented as an article, whereas people are inclined to ignore adverts. You may be able to include an article on the same page as your advertisement.

Professional journals often publish special editions or special interest supplements, so it can be particularly beneficial to advertise in one of these, if they tie in with your particular product. For example, *Training Journal,* published by Fenman in the UK, published an edition that was devoted to customer service training, so training providers that specialise in customer service training advertised in this issue. They knew that they were even more likely to be seen by the right people.

Internet advertising

Internet advertising is a relatively new medium and a very versatile one. Banner advertising has become very popular but there are regular reports in the press about how low 'click through' rates are calling into question the effectiveness of this medium. Many web users find this commercial interference annoying and ignore it. So the second generation of banner advertisements are bigger and bolder than before, using bright colours and shapes in a 3D effect so that, for example, blobs of colour come rushing towards the you and splat on the screen in front of you!

Matching medium to audience demands that the marketer considers a number of criteria, including campaign aims and objectives, ability to reach the audience and creative ability of the medium.

Creating effective advertising copy

Even if correctly positioned, an advertisement is only as good as its message or content. If it fails to create impact and attract the right kind of attention, the target audience will not see or hear it. When preparing effective advertising copy some rules to consider are:

Headline.	■ Must attract attention and appeal to self-interest to encourage the consumer to get involved and to read on or listen actively. ■ Use something that is new to the audience if possible. ■ Certain words and phrases attract attention, such as 'free', 'bargain', 'the last chance', 'the amazing truth about' – avoid being too sensational; be appropriate. ■ Include the brand. ■ Tell consumers what the selling line is.
Body copy.	■ Can be any style but must be appropriate and not offend. ■ Ensure it is easy to understand and provides enough information to encourage action. ■ Support the message with testimonials, helpful advice, facts and figures etc. ■ Use language that the audience understands.

Figure 9.1: Creating good advertising copy

Use the headline to provide information – brand name, product benefit etc., but try not to be too clever or mysterious because people will get bored. There is a fine balance between stimulating interest through doing something that is different and switching people off. You do not have much time to grab attention and create interest.

The body copy must add to their interest and begin to create desire to respond to the message.

Test out your advertisement on representatives of the target audience to gauge reaction and understanding.

Some advertisements in the past have caused offence but it is difficult to give some hard and fast rules about how this happens because audience reaction is not limited to what people see. Each person will interpret a message according to their experience of the world and make judgements based on his/her value sets about any controversial issues contained in the message. What offends one person might be amusing to another. The Advertising Standards Agency takes complaints from members of the public about advertisements that are misleading or offensive.

Communicating creatively through advertising

You may have observed some or all of the following tactics:

Short dramas or 'slice of life'

A short drama is performed using the product in a situation that the target audience is familiar with. On UK television, Flash cleaning products are used to solve common family cleaning problems (greasy stove, grimy bathroom) and a comparison is made with the hard work it would be without the product.

Aspirational

Used to create associations with brand on luxury items such as cars or expensive perfume. The consumer is encouraged to enter the same fantasy by purchasing the product.

Celebrity endorsement

Cosmetics and food and drink advertising often employ a 'famous name' to encourage consumers to 'act' like their heroes or heroines. The association must be positive and appropriate and the celebrity must be carefully chosen to have widespread appeal and not be involved in any controversy, because association can work both ways and if the audience does not like the celebrity for any reason, they will associate the product with this dislike.

Humour

Effective when used unexpectedly, such as in advertisements for financial services or utilities. Humour personalises what might otherwise be considered a dry or boring subject. However, the advertisement will be seen a number of times so the humour must be sustainable. In the UK the government used a scruffy housekeeper from a popular sitcom to tell people to complete self-assessment tax forms. Caution should be exercised in using humour because of the danger of trivialising the brand or making the audience take the product less seriously.

Product demonstration

Commonly used for gardening and healthcare products. The viewer is shown how easy they are to use and the benefits they could enjoy. UK advertisements for hearing aids and stair lifts use this technique. The key figure giving the demonstration might be a celebrity or the Chief Executive of the company.

Briefing an advertising agency

Most organisations use an advertising agency for design work. Even if you have built up a good relationship with key personnel within the agency so they understand the business you are in and your company vision and values, you should provide a full creative brief at the start of each campaign. This should include:

- Campaign aims and objectives and how they fit with existing marketing activities.
- Target audience and characteristics.
- Relevant company information – image, values, corporate colours and style etc.
- Key message – what you want to say.
- Product information – Unique Selling Point (USP), why customers buy etc.
- Media.
- Budget.
- Timescale.

Get to know the agency well before you employ them. Different agencies have different 'styles', some of which may not be appropriate for your product or service.

Planning an advertising campaign

Figure 9.2 shows the basic steps that marketers use when planning an advertising campaign:

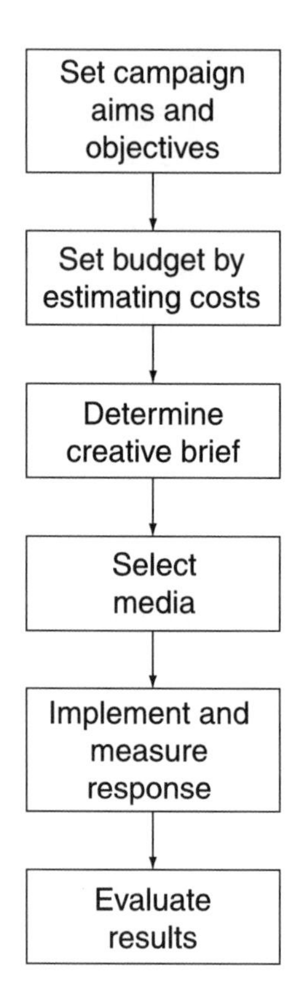

Figure 9.2: Planning an advertising campaign

When selecting media the main criteria are reach, coverage and feasibility – does the medium provide the right creative environment and is it appropriate for the brand and organisation? If using more than one medium a decision needs to be made on which one should be the main medium.

Having taken a decision on which medium or media to use, the planner then needs to prepare a schedule (e.g. on a Gantt chart) so each medium is used at the right time and in the right way. The planner must also check that all required resources are available.

Activity 9.1: Team presentation

You and a colleague, as Advertising Executives for your organisation or college, have been tasked with giving a 30-minute presentation to a group of new students about Internet advertising.

Write some brief notes to help you plan the content of the presentation.

Direct marketing

Targeted messages, sent to people who are most likely to respond, are an effective way to communicate. Targeting is a cost-effective factor in direct marketing because knowing the customer well enables the marketer to design messages that are more likely to get a response.

General messages for mass circulation may lack focus and appeal to nobody. The term viral marketing has sprung into use because of the practice of texting or emailing messages to untargeted groups with the expectation that some will be passed on.

Maintaining an effective relationship with customers means that organisations need to communicate regularly. However, they need to understand what preferences customers have for how that communication should be managed. For example, after purchase, immediate sales calls to check satisfaction are usually welcomed but further calls are more likely to be tolerated if they also remind customers that a purchase, such as a car, is due for servicing or giving other useful advice. This level of personal service is much more costly than direct mailshots or viral marketing, but the results are measurable, so their cost-effectiveness can be evaluated.

Direct mail

Direct mail, or 'junk mail' as it is sometimes referred to by recipients, is a common and cheap tool used by marketers to promote their products and services. Unfortunately, much of it is poorly targeted and can cause annoyance. Recent legislation means that consumers can actively choose not to receive unsolicited mail. These are rights which are gradually being enshrined in privacy and data protection legislation in many countries.

The potential advantages of direct mail are:

- Campaigns can be planned and implemented relatively quickly compared to other forms of promotion.
- The sophistication of customer databases mean that accurate targeting is possible, so it can be a cost-effective communication.
- Messages can be personalised.
- Letters can contain a great deal of detail about the many benefits that are available to consumers.
- It is measurable through registering response rates (email) or by using a reference number on a coupon.

Direct mail is used in both b2b and b2c markets to stimulate sales, gather names for the customer database, obtain sales leads and promote special offers. There are many different forms of direct mail including:

Direct mail letters.	A common form of promotion that informs consumers of a special offer or the launch of a new product. Car dealerships mail out details of new launches to their customers, often inviting them to a special preview event. Also widely used by charities because it is a relatively inexpensive way of getting their name in front of potential donors. You will have received many such mailings, so read the next few that come through your letterbox to assess how well they are constructed and whether they have been effectively targeted.
Flyers and leaflets.	Sometimes mailed or may be delivered by hand. Not personalised but a cheap way of mass marketing. May be more effective if combined with a sales promotion including a sample or money-off voucher.

Direct mail catalogues.	Many organisations sell via mail order, sending out unsolicited brochures to consumers. Charities use this method to sell to existing members. Brochures and catalogues are usually sent twice a year with incentives for the first purchase.
Email.	Increasingly used due to the relatively low cost compared with postal mailshots. Can be measured by linking to a web site and measuring the click through rate. Again, unsolicited emails can cause offence and consumers must be offered the opportunity to 'unsubscribe'. The format of these may be as an advertisement or take the form of a newsletter or bulletin.

Figure 9.3: Examples of direct mail

One of the critical success factors for direct mail, apart from accurate targeting, is making it easy for consumers to respond. If they have to read through lots of complicated instructions, they are unlikely to do anything but throw the mailshot away. Most mail order catalogues give customers the option of ordering by post, telephone or online so they can choose the process that is most convenient for them.

Activity 9.2: Briefing

As mentioned above, car dealerships often use direct mailings to communicate with customers.

Imagine that you are the Marketing Manager for such an organisation and have decided to have some leaflets and flyers printed promoting lower prices for new cars.

What information should be included in the brief to your local print and design agency to enable them to prepare a quotation?

Discuss your answer with fellow students who have experience of this kind of work.

Activity 9.3: Legal muscles from Brussels

Read the following short extract from an article that appeared in *Marketing Business,* September 2000.

"UK marketers also need to be aware of EU restrictions on sales promotions and direct marketing. The 1998 Data Protection Act, which originated from Brussels, includes new codes which affect direct marketing. Consumers can now deny future direct communications from a company and any third party it may pass their details on to. Previously, they could only opt out of third party communication.

If you want to know more about the EU legislation and codes of conduct for direct marketing and implications for the planning and organising of sales promotions, visit www.europa.eu.int or www.dma.org.uk (Direct Marketing Association)."

Consider the implications for marketers planning direct mailings.

Case Study – Consumer turn-off for TV ads

Consumers from nine European countries and the US believe advertising has increased significantly across all media during the last five years, according to a survey by CIA Sensor, a media communication company. TV ads are the ones consumers are keenest to avoid. The survey represents consumers' evaluations of the amount of advertising that they are exposed to, rather than an objective measure of it.

Overall, more people avoid ads related to buying than claim to be inspired by them. Across markets, magazines and newspapers provide more inspiration than avoidance, whilst the reverse is generally true in TV, with notable exceptions in the UK, Ireland and Italy. All three of these countries enjoy higher levels of advertising inspiration. Of the ten markets surveyed, the UK also had the second-lowest level of ad avoidance.

The nature of the ad medium affects the degree of ad avoidance, the survey found. For example, although TV is engaging, ads seem more intrusive. The remote control also gives consumers greater avoidance opportunities. However, when radio is used as a background to an activity the ads seem less intrusive. When print ads match content, readers tend to perceive a relevant message in the ads and therefore are less likely to regard them negatively.

In the case of TV, an average of 45% across all countries try to avoid the ads. In countries where TV advertising is heaviest, namely Italy and Spain, the avoidance levels are also highest, at 76% and 69% respectively. Italians view around 700 ads per week, while Spaniards see over 600. CIA suggests shorter but more frequent ad breaks may be a way round the problem.

It is not all bad news for TV advertisers, however. TV comes out top among consumers as the best source of inspiration for purchases, with print advertising following closely behind. In a number of countries where Internet penetration is high – the UK, Germany and the US – it is also regarded as a good source of shopping ideas.

Source: *Marketing Business,* December/January 2002.

Questions

As a Marketing Executive, write a memo report to your Manager about the survey findings.

SUMMARY OF KEY POINTS

- Mass media advertising is known as above-the-line promotion.
- Advertising is used by marketers to inform, influence and persuade at different stages of the product life cycle.
- Advertising is more effective when used in conjunction with other elements of the mix, for example sales promotion and selling.
- Effective copy combines a headline that draws the consumer in and body copy that prompts them to respond.
- Direct mail is most effective when accurately targeted and it is easy for the consumer to respond.
- It is used in all market sectors due to the cost-effectiveness and ease of implementation.
- It can be viewed as 'junk' or nuisance mail and marketers need to plan their campaigns within the requirements of data protection and privacy legislation.

Improving and developing own learning

The following projects are designed to help you to develop your knowledge and skills further by carrying out some research yourself. Feedback is not provided for this type of learning because there are no 'answers' to be found, but you may wish to discuss your findings with colleagues and fellow students.

Project A

You are the Advertising Manager for your favourite brand of chocolate or alcohol.

Plan a campaign to remind consumers about your brand.

What would the advertisement look like?

Where would it be seen?

Who would it be aimed at?

How could you evaluate success?

Project B

As Fund-raising Manager for your favourite charity, write a direct mail letter to people who have donated gifts in the past.

In the letter, ask them to support your latest fund-raising appeal.

Project C

Collect as many print advertisements as you can.

Review their effectiveness.

Carry out some research by asking friends and family which ads they have seen recently.

Feedback on activities

Activity 9.1: Team Presentation

Your notes might look something like this:

Introduction

- Introduce yourselves and explain your role regarding Internet advertising (establishing credibility).
- Explain presentation objectives:
  - To introduce the Internet as an advertising medium.
  - To explore potential benefits.
  - To discuss current practice.
  - To compare with print and broadcast advertising.
  - To discuss the future for Internet advertising.
- Outline presentation approach (presentation format, use of handouts, visual aids, etc.).
- Explain who will be leading each section of the presentation.
- Explain when questions can be asked.
- Set the scene – create opening impact and lead into…

Main body of presentation

- Explain the growth of Internet advertising (using examples), when it was first used and the medium characteristics.
- Compare the Internet as a medium with print and broadcast media – creative potential, cost, etc. etc.
- Describe the potential opportunities that the Internet offers advertisers, such as improved targeting and response rates, and the ability to measure effectiveness, now and in the future.
- Discuss barriers to effectiveness – poor design of advertisements, intrusive nature of banner ad, pop-up menus, etc.
- Compare design of web, print and broadcast advertisements (with examples).
- Encourage interaction by asking audience to comment on examples they have seen.

Summary

- Summarise main points to show how presentation objectives have been met.
- Create impact at the close.
- Ask for questions but have some prepared in case none are forthcoming.
- Re-summarise if necessary.

Activity 9.2: Briefing

If using a local print and design agency you may discuss the design with them and request they prepare some creative proofs. In order to obtain a quote, the brief should contain the following information:

- Aims and objectives – the purpose of the mailing.
- Relevant product information.
- Characteristics of the target groups to determine style, approach.
- The message.
- Other information.
- Size of the leaflet or flyer.
- Quality of paper.

- Quantity required.
- Volume of copy.
- Number of pictures/photographs.
- Colour requirements.
- Quality of material.
- Delivery date.
- A rough mock-up of the final product.

Activity 9.3: Legal muscles from Brussels

There is a lot of information available on new legislation being introduced on the two web sites. However, marketers should be aware that different rules and customs will be in force in different countries in the world. Some countries are more relaxed than the UK but generally it is not good practice to send unsolicited mail without permission. Consumers who are inundated with such mail may become very switched off. The new legislation is designed to give consumers greater protection from such annoyance.

Session 10

Displays and exhibitions

Introduction

This practical review of display materials and exhibitions reveals how many different opportunities there are to communicate with customers. Since displays and exhibitions should be part of an integrated communications campaign, this Session should be studied in conjunction with the other Sessions on the tools of the marketing mix and not considered as a stand-alone guide to promoting products and services in-store and at exhibitions.

LEARNING OUTCOMES

At the end of this Session you will be able to:

- Explain the role of Point of Sale (POS) materials and how they are developing in response to changing customer needs.
- Describe different types of display materials and design considerations.
- Discuss the role of exhibitions as a communications tool and their role in promotions.
- Discuss the effective use of display materials at exhibitions.

Point of sale material

Display materials and merchandising are used in-store to grab attention and persuade consumers to buy. Little text is used but the brand image is prominent and may be linked to a current advertising campaign. 'Eye-catching' displays are exactly that – designed at eye level so they are easily seen by shoppers wandering round the store.

In-store displays are becoming bigger and bolder to attract attention. They may be stand-alone units designed to hold stock or material that can be incorporated into the store's own display system. Materials used in temporary displays are usually paper-based but many have special print effects including laminated panels and holograms. More permanent displays might be made of plastic material and revolve around a central axis or have moveable shelves so the display can be refreshed. Mobile displays that hang from ceilings are rarely used for temporary displays but often used by stores as permanent store guides to products.

The placement of the display can also influence potential sales. Confectionery displays are often near checkouts, so consumers pick up the product as an impulse buy. Other items will be placed appropriately where adjacent items might stimulate sales. End-of-aisle displays in supermarkets are effective because the product is more isolated and therefore attracts more attention to itself.

In order to be effective, displays must be appropriately placed, attract attention, display the product effectively, promote the brand and be kept clean by staff!

Merchandising

The way products are displayed on shelves influences the decision to purchase. Related products should be displayed together so consumers will buy all that are appropriate, instead of a single item. For example, washing powders and fabric conditioners are stacked adjacent to each other so one acts as a reminder of the other. Each manufacturer requires all their flavours of jam to be together to encourage the consumer to buy their three favourites from that one brand.

The amount of shelf space is not the only factor to consider – the product must be displayed in the correct location on the shelf. Think about the trips you make to a supermarket or bookstore and browse along the shelves. Where do you look first. Usually middle of the shelf at eye level. How often do you pick up a book from the lower shelves first?

Brand owners often employ their own merchandisers or use their sales force to visit each outlet that stocks their products to organise the display, so the brand image is correctly displayed, and to restock if appropriate. The salesperson will negotiate with the store to secure the best location for the products he/she is selling.

Alternatively, manufacturers might provide strict guidelines to the store on how the product should be displayed and will periodically check that these guidelines are adhered to. Free merchandising is often provided as a trade incentive to stock products or take display stands.

The next Session discusses how brands are used to communicate with customers.

Merchandising and POS tools

Stores use a number of different merchandising tools and point of sales materials to attract attention, including:

- Window displays – usually fairly simple compared to ten years ago.
- Shelf stickers with a simple message.
- Posters and showcards that may be hung from the ceiling.
- Branded display units.
- Three dimensional units that may revolve.
- Interactive units that consumers can use for information on current special promotions.
- Manufacturers also use bold colours and patterns on the product packaging so it presents a block of colour to the browser – colour blocking. Packaging is discussed in the next Session.
- Shelf positioning as already discussed.
- In-store announcements on a public address system.
- Bins – products piled up rather than neatly displayed.

Next time you are shopping, look at the tools that the store has used and note how effective each one is.

Activity 10.1: Merchandising

Carry out some research into merchandising by visiting your local supermarket and walking around the shelves.

Note which brands are effectively displayed and which are very visible.

How many different tools – mentioned above – have been used?

Compare your list with other people's.

Exhibitions

Exhibitions represent a good opportunity for organisations to communicate face to face with customers. There are many types of exhibition, some of which are briefly described below. Selecting the right exhibition depends on gathering accurate information on who is likely to attend and understanding the message the business is trying to get across.

Advanced publicity may contribute to the success of exhibiting at shows due to the intensity of competition. Most organisations do this by sending invitations to regular clients via their sales force or by letter. The exhibition stand must be visual, memorable and encourage the visitor to interact with the organisation and its products and services.

To maximise communication and sales opportunities:

- Have a good product or service and a clear message to promote.
- Ensure you have an attractive entry in the exhibition catalogue.
- Check which journals and broadcast media are previewing the exhibition and provide the editors with all relevant information. Invite relevant journalists to visit your stand. The exhibition press office usually handles these arrangements.
- Develop a good relationship with the exhibition press officer who can provide information about arrangements for the press day, details of the official opener and their background and exhibition newsletters. If the VIP party has an interest in your products and services, propose that your stand is included in the official tour. Provide clear and concise press packs for journalists. Ensure you know how many press releases are allowed and keep in daily contact with the press office during the exhibition.
- Check the day before that the stand has arrived been erected correctly and that all printed materials and giveaways are displayed. Make sure all boxes and rubbish is cleared away.
- The press office will issue information to exhibitors daily about events that are scheduled for that day or the next. This bulletin provides an excellent PR opportunity.
- Train stand staff to interact effectively with visitors and ensure they have up to date product knowledge.
- Follow up sales leads immediately.
- Keep a record of all customer contacts made during the exhibition for future reference.
- Follow up all press leads. If your stand or products were featured then contact the relevant editors to discuss possible follow up article or interviews.

b2b trade shows

Business to business exhibitions are exactly what the name suggests. They attract specific media interest, often from the trade press, because they are specific to one industry such as hotel and catering or the water industry, for example. The relevant trade journals will have pre- and post-exhibition reports so there are additional opportunities for PR activities in addition to promoting products and services at the exhibition.

b2c trade shows

Consumer trade shows are industry-specific and examples include National Motor Show, Ideal Homes Exhibition and Holiday and Leisure Show. It is an opportunity to meet a wider audience than usual and gather feedback from existing customers face to face. To encourage sales many exhibitors offer special show discounts on products and services if purchased at the event.

Not-for-profit sector exhibitions

These are normally exhibitions for suppliers to specific sectors such as charities, voluntary organisations and local government.

Virtual exhibitions

The cost of exhibiting can be considerable so increasingly exhibition organisers offer the opportunity for exhibitors to take part in a virtual exhibition on the Internet. The advantage is that information posted is right up to date and the exhibition usually remains 'live' for a few weeks rather than a few days.

Mobile exhibition or roadshow

Much smaller than a static exhibition, a mobile exhibition or roadshow can be set up in customers' premises or a hotel room. They are usually staged for a specific purpose such as brand promotion, or building awareness of a public service such as breast screening.

Conferences

Conferences come in many different types and formats but they are usually staged to get like-minded people together to hear keynote speakers and discuss topical and relevant issues. Examples include an organisation's national sales conference, an international conference on global warming where delegates include politicians and environmental experts or a conference organised by a professional body for members and officials. There are often opportunities for companies in the industry to exhibit at conferences and for specialists to present papers (a PR opportunity).

Seminars

Seminars fulfil a similar purpose to conferences, but are smaller and shorter events. They may take the form of a breakfast, lunch or evening seminar for business people or one run by a charity to discuss issues with volunteers or other public bodies. It is a common method of communicating with stakeholders in the business and the not-for-profit sectors.

Activity 10.2: Measuring effectiveness

As Marketing Manager, write a memo to your staff explaining the importance of exhibitions in achieving company sales objectives.

Exhibition stands

You may have attended exhibitions full of good intentions to visit a number of stands to gather information about products and services that you might use in the future, only to be disappointed by the poor display on show. No opportunity is made to engage by the staff and you pass by determined to give that organisation a wide berth in the future.

Previous Sessions have explored the benefits of effective face to face communication but what about the messages communicated by the stand and the display? What impression of the brand and organisation are they communicating?

To ensure a positive impression is made:

- Make sure staff, stand and displays are clean and tidy.
- Ensure staff are fresh and alert, not tired and bored.
- Do not eat and drink on the stand.
- Find ways of 'involving' visitors in your products and services through interactive displays, videos, competitions, quizzes, demonstrations and fun stunts.

- Make good use of the space so people can move around.
- Talk to visitors to find out why they are interested in your organisation and make sure they go away with relevant information.
- Push the brand appropriately – freebies, carrier bags, stickers – but do not use a 'hard sell' approach; rather listen, learn and respond.

There are very few opportunities to get face to face with customers so make the most of it!

Activity 10.3: I can't hear you!

You have been selected to represent your company at an international exhibition. Write some notes to remind yourself about barriers to effective communication and how they might be overcome.

Case Study – Bulletin PR

Reuters photojournalist, Anthony Hayward set up Bulletin ten years ago. Now it has a team of 75 and offices in London, Singapore, Kuala Lumpur, Melbourne, Sydney, New York and Paris.

Together, Lotus and Bulletin planned a promotional campaign to cover the launch of the Lotus M250 model at the Frankfurter motor show. "It was quite a challenge to grab share of the media coverage," says Hayward, "especially given Lotus's small spend at the motor show compared to other manufacturers."

Bulletin targeted TV news and features programmes in five European countries. It also went after 25 news and lifestyle web sites. "Its important to be quick off the mark to broadcast what they are looking for," says Hayward, "We distributed the first satellite feed of the day which helped put Lotus at the forefront of the news coverage of the show. The result was two and a half hours' TV coverage, 50 press reports across our target countries, a cumulative audience of more than 48 million, and online reports which attracted more than 80 million impressions."

But behind that day's filming and broadcast lie weeks, if not months of planning. Evaluation of the project – gleaned form an intricate analysis looking at coverage time, message delivery, quality of target audience achieved and other factors – showed that Lotus got its key messages across in 69% of comment; it achieved

10% share of voice in coverage of the show; it received 80 deposits for the M250 as a result; and it had two enquiries for engineering contracts.

The approach for BMW's haute couture fashion show in the Middle East was different.

"It would not have worked simply to apply traditional PR practices to this campaign because the cultures of Middle Eastern countries are so individual," says Hayward. "The strategy had to incorporate differing attitudes to PR by Middle Eastern broadcasters."

Instead BMW benefited from the region's more relaxed approach to product mentions. BMW had worked with Bulletin since 1991 – on projects from financial results and plant openings to corporate sponsorship. This time, in the Middle East, the aim was to maximise regional exposure by communicating synergy between the BMW brand and haute couture and increasing sales.

The result was six hours, 33 minutes of coverage with 42 reports and a cumulative audience of 6.5 million – worth a comparative advertising spend of 1 million US dollars.

Of all the coverage BMW received for the event, 88% was generated by Bulletin; 86% credited BMW. Regional sales rose 35% during the campaign and 45 out of 50 special edition cars prepared for the event were sold during the tour.

So how much does all this cost? Inevitably it varies, campaign by campaign. But, as an example, a 15-country campaign would come in at about £100-£150K – budgets Hayward finds tend to come out of advertising spend rather than from PR.

So, is it more valuable than advertising? "Both have their place and work well together," says Hayward. "Advertising guarantees exposure, whereas PR's strength is its credibility. "

Source: *Marketing Business,* April 2000.

Questions

1. What lessons can you learn from the information in the Case Study about successful PR at exhibitions?
2. What does Hayward think are the relative merits of advertising and PR in terms of communication?
3. How were the results of the Lotus exhibition measured?

SUMMARY OF KEY POINTS

- In-store displays can be very effective ways of presenting products to consumers.
- Manufacturers like to maintain some control over how their products are displayed so may provide marketing and merchandising support free of charge.
- Effective merchandising can significantly increase the number of products bought by a consumer by placing relevant products adjacent to each other.
- Exhibitions are an excellent opportunity to get face to face with existing customers and consumers.
- The opportunities to communicate with different groups at exhibitions are many and varied but need to be carefully managed.
- Make a positive impression at exhibitions – you never know who is passing by.

Improving and developing own learning

The following projects are designed to help you to develop your knowledge and skills further by carrying out some research yourself. Feedback is not provided for this type of learning because there are no 'answers' to be found, but you may wish to discuss your findings with colleagues and fellow students.

Project A

Look at the displays in your local shops and supermarkets.

How effectively are products displayed?

Which ones have caught your eye? Why?

What improvements can you make for your favourite brands?

Project B

Imagine that you are designing a stand for your organisation at a national exhibition.

What would you do to ensure that you maximise the opportunities to communicate with your target audience?

Project C

Consider recent exhibitions that you have attended.

Which organisations made a positive impression? Why was this?

Which organisations made a poor impression? Why was this?

If you have not attended an exhibition, do some research amongst friends and colleagues who have attended one recently.

Feedback on activities

Activity 10.1: Merchandising

You will probably be most aware of the brands that:

- Are displayed at eye level.
- Are displayed end-of-aisle.

- Produce blocks of colour such as Cadbury's Dairy Milk chocolate (purple).
- Have special offers prominently displayed on their packaging.
- Have recently been advertised effectively.

Activity 10.2: Measuring effectiveness

Internal Memorandum

To: Marketing Team
From: Jules Freeboard, Marketing Manager

Date: 15 July 200X

Subject: Importance of exhibitions

As we are now planning for the international Toy Fair in November, I am sending this reminder of the importance for the company of having a strong presence at exhibitions.

Exhibitions contribute towards the achievement of company sales objectives by:

- Offering an opportunity to meet face to face with customers to gather information about how well we are meeting their needs and how those needs might change in the future.
- Providing an opportunity to see what the competition are doing to promote their products.
- Allowing us to meet potential customers to find out why they do not buy our products at present.
- Allowing us to present full product and new product ranges to customers.
- Enable us to promote our products internationally through effective use of PR.
- Strengthening branding and reinforcing corporate image.

I look forward to discussing this with you further at our next planning meeting on 20 July 200X

Activity 10.3: I can't hear you!

Barriers to overcome include:

Barrier	**How to overcome barrier**
Physical noise.	■ Speak clearly and distinctly. ■ Select quieter positions for discussion. ■ Move away from other conversations to avoid distractions. ■ Use good eye contact.
Boredom.	■ If visitors do not appear interested find out what their needs are and present relevant solutions. ■ Appear alert and interested myself.
Language.	■ Avoid using technical terms and jargon unless appropriate. ■ Some international visitors may not speak my language so be aware of who can speak different foreign languages on our team.

Session 11

Corporate image and branding

Introduction

In order to encourage loyalty and repeat business, organisations need to ensure that their products are attractive to, and recognised by, customers. Therefore they need to create an identity and 'personality' for that brand. Activities that effectively develop and build a brand are critical to success and help support the logo and other visual aspects of the brand.

This Session explores how organisations develop their image, establish brands and communicate them to customers.

LEARNING OUTCOMES

At the end of this Session you will be able to:

- Explain what is meant by corporate image and identity.
- Discuss the reasons why branding is important to organisations.
- Discuss the purpose of logos and symbols used by organisations to identify themselves.
- Explain the role of corporate identity, brand image and logos in corporate communication with customers.
- Explain the role of packaging in the promotions mix.

Corporate image

The visual image, the corporate logo and colours, are all important parts of the communication with customers. Just think for a moment about the instantly recognisable symbols such as the Michelin man and the form of writing used by Kellogg's. However, the image that we have of an organisation is not simply a visual one – although we may picture the corporate logo or staff uniform when we talk about it – it also encompasses the reputation of that company. The image that we have of McDonald's is not simply the big yellow arches, but perhaps the impression that the service is good and the restaurants are always clean.

Image and reputation are the elements which make an organisation familiar to us, and which help give it an identity that we recognise when we see a picture or symbol associated with it or hear others talking about it. Identity 'individualises' organisations so we can distinguish one from another. This is particularly important for products that are similar or positioned close together on shelves in shops.

Organisations select corporate colours, logos and symbols that are consistent with the identity they wish to communicate. An upmarket company might select burgundy or purple because it is a rich colour, whereas an organisation at the budget end of the market might go for a cheap and cheerful bright colour. Before selection, companies will test out the image that their logo and symbols convey to their stakeholders using different colours, graphics, sizes and shapes.

The way corporate and brand logos are used by organisations often differs from country to country. American culture expects a logo to be large and prominent, whereas the French prefer logos on clothes to be quite discreet. The use of certain colours for POS material and packaging can also be tricky. Packaging that uses red and yellow may cause offence to patriots in Spain because these are colours in the national flag. Purple should be avoided in Greece because it is associated with funerals.

When you have completed the first activity in this Session, you will appreciate that there are many opportunities for organisations to communicate identity, so messages must be congruent. There are also many opportunities for organisations to damage their image (and reputation). If they present themselves in the media as a caring organisation but their staff appear otherwise, then the image will be damaged. Unfortunately, bad news is news and travels fast – as discussed in the Case Study for Session 8.

Activity 11.1: What do you see?

What are the means that an organisation uses to communicate visually to its markets in order to build its identity?

Discuss several different organisations with fellow students and colleagues to see how your images of the same organisations compare. Discuss any differences you have.

You will find that personal experience and knowledge of how that organisation has dealt with others will add to your attitude towards the organisation and how you regard its reputation.

Corporate literature

Corporate literature includes stationery, catalogues, brochures, leaflets, notices, business cards and other printed materials produced by the company to communicate with stakeholders. It should have a consistent appearance to help reinforce image so corporate colours are used and other logos and symbols that aid recognition.

As a marketer, if you work on corporate communications, you will be aware of how much detail goes into the production of corporate literature. The company will use specific typefaces, layout, colours, logo in the same position, addresses and contact details in the same position and other design techniques to ensure that it is instantly recognisable. In larger companies, these will all be defined in a house style manual to ensure consistency. Companies will make great efforts to control the use of their logos and brands by third parties.

Corporate web site

The Internet has provided a new opportunity for organisations to reach their stakeholders. However, many organisations fail through poor planning or design to make the most of this opportunity to communicate. To make the right impression, companies should consider the following factors:

- Who will be accessing it and what information you want to share with them. The content of the web site should be specific to the needs of the users.
- The purpose of the communication which might include some or all of the following:

- Promotion of products and services.
- Online sales.
- Online services.
- Communication of company background to establish image and reputation.
- Provision of information to stakeholders including the annual report.
- Recruitment.
- Development of brands.
- Opportunity to gather feedback from customers and users.

- How it will be maintained and kept up to date.
- Accurately representing company logo and identity so existing customers recognise the site. Changing the image for the Internet may confuse and lead to lost customers. Many organisations go 'over the top' on design and include flashy features that conflict with their normal image and frustrate users who simply want information.
- Ease of navigation. Putting a navigation bar on every page reminds the user of what is available and means that they can access the information they want in a few clicks. A 'top of the page' button also saves the user time.
- Piloting to ensure that the web site is user friendly. Making it easy to use will enhance good customer relationships and the image of customer care.
- Opportunity for users to contact the company, such as an email contact.
- Encouraging repeat visits by offering something free and making sure that the site is regularly updated.

Activity 11.2: Web works

Visit the following museum web sites and use the above checklist to review the facilities offered and presentation of information.

How user friendly do you think they are?

i. www.vam.ac.uk – Victoria and Albert Museum in London.

ii. www.rmbr.nus.edu.sg/ – Museum of Biodiversity in Singapore.

Packaging

Packaging is an important and significant promotional tool for marketers. Many organisations use corporate colours in their packaging to aid recognition and make sure that the logo is prominently displayed. If you go to the supermarket, note how certain brands stand out on the shelves because of the colour of their packaging. This phenomenon is referred to as colour blocking. Packaging is referred to as the silent salesman because it helps sell the product through aiding recognition and provision of information.

By law, packaging must include such information as weight of product, ingredients, nutritional values and relevant health warnings, so that it aids the consumer in their information search. For example, a consumer looking for a low-calorie ready-made meal can compare price, fat content and range of ingredients when searching for alternatives. Details of special offers and price discounts are also often communicated via packaging.

The power of branding

Successful branding is the result of building an identity that customers instantly recognise, associate with a certain quality and feel loyal to, so they show a preference for that brand. Brand identity is communicated via:

- Brand mark such as logo and symbol (e.g. the Macintosh apple).
- Specific design and colours used (strong red and yellow colours used by McDonald's, and their yellow arches).
- Trademark.
- Brand name or words (Coca-Cola is recognisable in whichever language it is presented in, because of the design of the words).

Branding creates a 'personality' that customers who prefer that brand relate to. It distinguishes one brand from another. For example, for many years PG Tips used chimps in their advertisements to promote their tea bags, and Andrex use puppies in their advertisements for toilet paper.

Branding encourages association in consumers' minds so they can differentiate individual brands. That may be done through a phrase used to promote the product. Kit-Kat uses 'Have a break, have a Kit-Kat' in order that consumers will think of this chocolate bar at 'break times'. In conjunction with the strong red packaging which has changed little over the years, this has led to strong recognition so consumers loyal to this brand will think of Kit-Kat when they go to buy a bar of chocolate.

Creating a successful brand identity involves ensuring consumers develop a positive attitude towards the product and wish to identify themselves with it. Martini created a jet-set image for their products by using a series of advertisements that depicted a famous actress enjoying the drink while travelling on an aeroplane. By association consumers 'indulge' in the 'jet-set lifestyle' by drinking Martini!

Brand awareness

Creating brand awareness means informing consumers about the brand and reinforcing recognition. The brand must be easily recognisable and 'seen in all the right places'. It needs to be associated with people, objects and organisations that share common characteristics, so that a consistent message is communicated.

What individuals see and feel when they encounter the brand is important. Visual elements of the brand are one way of taking in information about the brand but emotions that are felt on seeing the brand create a 'feeling' for the brand. A 'feel good' factor may contribute to the growth of confidence in a brand and the organisation.

Marketers use lots of different tools and techniques to create brand awareness and build a positive image:

- Celebrity endorsement.
- Sponsorship.
- PR activities.
- Corporate hospitality.
- Advertising.

Again, there are just as many opportunities to communicate brand identity as corporate identity, but just as many to get it wrong. If advertising offends, for example, then the customer's perception of the brand image is tarnished. If the celebrity falls from grace then the association is no longer beneficial.

The benefits of branding

Once a brand is established with strong recognition among consumers then the organisation may be able to extend or stretch the use of the brand into different market sectors. Virgin has created branded products in many different market sectors including fizzy drinks, financial services and railways. While this can benefit the company, as their products are recognised in different markets, there is disadvantage that failure in one sector may lead to damage to sales or image in another. This does not always follow. Organisations can protect their brand if they act wisely. Virgin trains do not have a good record as a top service provider but there is no evidence that this has affected other branded products.

Another example is easyJet airlines. The success of the brand encouraged the organisation to found easyEverything.com, cybercafés in Europe and New York, and easyRentacar.com. Notice the use of the brand design in the names of the new businesses. However, the brand name does not guarantee success – the cybercafés are not doing as well as anticipated.

What other examples can you think of?

Activity 11.3: A global brand for Vodafone

Read the short article that appeared in *Marketing Business,* March 2002, and answer the questions set:

Mobile communications company Vodafone is migrating its various brands around the globe under one name. The latest to make the move is Greek subsidiary, formerly Panafon, then Panafon-Vodafone for a year. It finally became Vodafone in January.

The dual branding strategy enables the Vodafone name to be introduced into local markets, building upon the brand equity of the local brand. Once established, operators migrate to the single brand. In Greece, 81% recognition and acceptance rating suggested the time was right to make the change.

"We are continuing to implement our global Vodafone brand recognition campaign ahead of migration to the single brand," said Thomas Geitner, Chief Executive, Global Products and Services, Vodafone Group plc.

Germany's Vodafone D2 will migrate to the single brand this month (March 2002), followed by Europolitan Vodafone in Sweden which is due to make the change in April. J-Phone in Japan is currently at the dual brand stage as are subsidiaries in Egypt, Ireland, Italy and the Netherlands, which are due to change to the single brand during the course of this year. Portuguese and Spanish subsidiaries made the move in October 2001.

Questions

1. How are Vodafone achieving brand recognition in global markets?
2. What else could they do to create greater brand awareness? Discuss this with fellow students or colleagues to increase your list.

Case Study – Tyres: the branding challenge

One of the few times people think about car tyres is when they go flat! And then they are seen as a big nuisance. So you would think that being the Marketing Director of a big car tyre company would not be quite as stimulating or diverting as doing the job for something you considered more glamorous – like the cars themselves for example. But you would be wrong.

At least that's the message from Antonio Betes, Sales and Marketing Director at the UK business of German tyre group Continental. Talking to Betes is not only an education in how what seems like a fairly straightforward sector can nevertheless be both complex and compelling. But it also shows how any business can benefit from someone who champions the principles of good, solid marketing.

What about the challenge of branding? How do you brand something that is perceived as, well, dull? Nonsense, declares Betes. "There are two things that you keep hearing from people in the tyre industry and which I firmly don't agree with. The first is that tyres are boring. Anything that costs as much as tyres is not boring."

The second is that they are a distress purchase. And it's easy to see why the trade believes that. After all, unlike any other consumer products, where you can go to the high street and buy something from any number of outlets and bring it home, you can't with tyres. They have to be fitted. There is no DIY when it comes to tyre fitting. So the trade plays a disproportionately large role in the route to the customer.

That has led to the trade in many instances having a 'wait until they turn up' approach to customer dealings. So Betes would like to see tyre dealers taking a much more proactive, marketing oriented stance. It's also necessary, he feels. "The world doesn't stay as comfortable forever. They have to become more competitive and start focusing on the next purchase, trying to lock customers in. You don't get future value or recognition if you are always looking at the market in a historical context like distress purchasing. If you do that, you will never look forward and tap potential. It's a two-pronged problem: the trade has to understand what your products are, and the consumer has to have some recognition and understanding of your brand. When consumers go to the tyre fitter and ask for a tyre, and the fitters recommend one, you want consumers to accept it because they have recognition and confidence in the brand. Whether we like it or not, it's the tyre fitters who are crucial."

So for the trade, the company carries out a lot of what Betes calls push activity, with things like incentive programmes and training and education to make sure they have a clear understanding of the 'brand ladder' or the different brand segments each one of the 11 on offer occupies.

The flagship brands, for example, are Continental – or Conti for short – in the premium sector and Uniroyal in the quality sector. There are also the economy and budget brands, and own label products. And some brands have been created to be exclusive to certain distributors. There's a lot to juggle with.

Even more of a challenge is to get consumers to think about tyres as anything other than those black objects attached to their cars. Continental began this branding journey for Conti a few years back with a five year sponsorship of the Champions league of the European Cup. That ended two years ago when it was decided that it was time to move the brand beyond that particular audience and broaden its awareness. Betes became part of a pan-European team to devise a new advertising strategy for the brand.

This resulted in a major new campaign for Conti in the Eurpoean market using both TV and press advertising. The core concept was adapted to each market according to language and culture, explains Betes – or 'glocalisation' as he puts it. In Germany, for example, the campaign has a harder edge, whereas in the UK it's softer and more droll. So the theme of 'taking care of the one you love' is followed by the punchline, '80% of men have a secret love affair – with their car.'

But he's not ignoring female consumers, particularly since they are now responsible for 40% of tyre purchases. In fact, to see how women would react to the campaign he ran women-only focus groups where the ads tested favourably. And he wants to build on that by putting much more emphasis on the sort of PR which will get more female awareness. That could include attention-grabbing surveys along the lines of, for instance, do men love their cars more than their wives? He knows that sort of survey could even get headlines in the tabloids. His eyes positively gleam at the thought.

Source: *Marketing Business,* December/January 2002.

Questions

1. What does Betes think is important for consumers to feel when offered a brand of tyre by fitters?
2. How is the Conti brand communicated to consumers?
3. What are the barriers faced by Betes to creating brand awareness and developing brand loyalty?

SUMMARY OF KEY POINTS

- Corporate identity is not only concerned with the visual presentation of the organisation, but also includes reputation.
- Corporate identity is communicated via company literature, promotional activities, web site, personnel, logos and other visual symbols.
- Successful branding leads to good recognition of the brand and loyalty.
- Marketers develop brands with 'personalities' to help consumers engage with that brand.
- Strong brands enable organisations to create a presence in new market sectors.

Improving and developing own learning

The following projects are designed to help you to develop your knowledge and skills further by carrying out some research yourself. Feedback is not provided for this type of learning because there are no 'answers' to be found, but you may wish to discuss your findings with colleagues and fellow students.

Project A

For your own organisation, or one you know well, list all the ways in which the organisation communicates its identity.

What improvements can you suggest?

Project B

Imagine that you are Brand Manager for a toilet roll manufacturer.

What tools and tactics would you use to create brand awareness and differentiate your brand from other top selling names such as Andrex?

(Most consumers recognise the Andrex puppies, used in advertising, giving the brand a strong presence in the market).

Project C

On your next few shopping trips look at product packaging to identify the different ways they have been used to promote the product.

What information is written on the package?

How does it aid product recognition?

Feedback on activities

Activity 11.1: What do you see?

- Corporate literature, printed materials and stationery.
- Logo.
- Staff uniforms.
- Delivery or transportation vehicles in corporate colours, with logo.
- Packaging.
- Corporate personnel at work and in the media.
- Results of news releases on TV and in print.
- Corporate web site.
- Office buildings, retail outlets, central office etc.

Activity 11.2: Web works

Having reviewed the web sites, what suggestions can you make to improve the way the organisations communicate with their users? You may have considered the following:

- Ease of navigation.
- Time taken to download.
- Content organisation – is it easy to find out where relevant information can be accessed?
- Use of white space – easy to read on screen?
- Can you email queries – and how quickly do they respond?
- Can you communicate with a human being if required?

Activity 11.3: A global brand for Vodafone

1. How are Vodafone achieving brand recognition in global markets?
   - By creating association with local brands and then migrating to a single brand status, enabling consumers to get used to a brand name change.

2. What else could they do to create greater brand awareness?
   - Use the logo in association with the local brand and then increase its presence elsewhere as below.
   - PR activities that present the brand locally.
   - Sponsor local activities, personalities.
   - Poster advertising using corporate colours and logo.

Session 12

New developments in customer communications

Introduction

This final Session reviews the information given throughout the Companion on the way technology is changing organisations' abilities to communicate with stakeholders and how they can look into the future. Examples are given but the rate of change of technology means that some of these will be out of date before this Companion is published. You are therefore, recommended to keep your reading of the marketing press up to date!

LEARNING OUTCOMES

At the end of this Session you will be able to:

- Explain the role of Information and Communications Technology (ICT) in communications, including digital TV and interactive marketing.
- Describe examples of the role of ICT in customer communications and how this is changing.
- Discuss how digital technology impacts on marketing activities and affects media decisions.

Changing communications

There are many different ways in which ICT has changed the way organisations communicate with different stakeholder groups:

- Email has become well established as a means of both internal and external communication, replacing memos and faxes in many instances.
- Mobile telephones have increased the capability of people to keep in touch on the move and the new Wireless Application Protocol (WAP) phones provide a full range of facilities, including Internet access, electronic services and games. (Visit www.wapforum.org, the web site for WAP Forum to find out more about WAP and industry standards).
- Laptop computers mean that field staff, such as salespeople, can keep in touch with their central office, sending and receiving messages, accessing training and other services.

- Laptop technology means that organisational personnel can take sophisticated presentations to clients that can be readily customised.
- Palmtops and electronic diaries mean that information is readily portable and new information can be downloaded onto a central PC system.
- WAP phones and the Internet can also be used as new advertising channels.
- Text messaging.
- The Internet provides new opportunities to communicate through corporate web sites, chat rooms and virtual networking groups.
- Many organisations have company Intranets for the internal distribution of company information.
- Parts of the company Intranet can be made available externally – an Extranet – so customers and suppliers can access specific information when they need it.
- Teleconferencing, videoconferencing and satellite connections enable people who are separated by distance and time to have a discussion in real time.
- Relational databases enable marketers to identify small market segments and target these groups with specific and personalised mailings.
- Interactive television enables consumers to shop at home and use the Internet without a PC.

Many examples of the above are referred to throughout this Companion.

Activity 12.1: Internet benefits

Consider the advantages that the Internet offers marketers as a communication channel.

Present this information in a table format.

Interacting with customers

Developments in the creative use of ICT have revolutionised the way marketers can interact with consumers. Company web sites provide email contact as standard, so consumers can send a query and receive an individual response.

Having collected information about consumers, they can then be sent relevant information about services and products that they may like. For example, when you purchase online, you will be sent details of related products that may also be of interest to you. Amazon.com keep their customers updated with the latest releases that 'match' previous purchases. Other sites offer services such as reminding you of important family birthdays so you can buy cards and gifts.

Online shopping sites are also looking for new technology to help them convert browsers into purchasers. One problem that has been identified as a barrier to purchase is the lack of personal contact. New technology is being developed that will enable the would-be shopper to click on a button that connects them to a call centre where they will receive individual attention to help them complete their purchase. The problem that marketers might face in trying to promote brands via online shopping sites is that consumers can personalise their sites so they only see the brands they want. Others can be vanished at the click of a mouse!

The next generation of web sites will include facilities for consumers to send in pictures or images of themselves so products can be specially selected for them. For example, consumers sending pictures of their hair or skin could have cosmetics matched to their skin or hair colour. Already new technology exists whereby the consumer and call centre agent can call up a virtual whiteboard and draw diagrams to aid explanations.

The new developments mean that marketers are having to experiment. But they are also going to have to use these new developments carefully if they do not want to annoy their customers. They also need to recognise and take into account the relevant privacy and data protection legislation.

The next sections, following Activity 12.2, explore some of the ways new technology is enabling marketers to get to know more about consumers, why and how they buy and the opportunities that exist to promote products and services.

Activity 12.2: Poppy site success

Read the following article which appeared in *Marketing Business,* March 2002.

"Poppy.org.uk, the web site created by the Royal British Legion as part of its annual poppy appeal, has doubled traffic in its second year with visitor numbers reaching almost 30,000.

Traffic has been driven to the site in a number of ways, including promotions on key search engines and an email campaign. 'Cold' emailing was experimented with and of 10,000 emails sent, 48 per cent were opened within days, achieving a click through rate of 5.4%.

Existing British Legion supporters were also emailed, and this achieved a 20% click through rate. Funds raised through the site go towards the Legion's work, which offers support on a wide range of welfare and resettlement issues to 15 million ex-Service people and their families. In 2000-1 the poppy appeal raised a total of 20.1 million."

List the different ways in which the Legion used ICT to promote their cause.

Electronic Point of Sale (EPOS)

EPOS enables supermarkets and stores to capture a great deal of information about their customers and their buying habits. Data from the EPOS system is also used to:

- Control stock more effectively due to the speed at which information is available.
- Inform shelf allocation and merchandising so consumers are encouraged to purchase more. How many times have you gone into a supermarket to buy a few items and come out with many more than you intended?

The level of competition between the most successful supermarket giants means that this information is invaluable to stores. It is difficult to gain customer loyalty because it is easy for them to shop elsewhere if they cannot purchase their favourite brand.

Text messaging

This is an increasingly popular way for organisations to inform consumers of sales promotions. First used mainly by telecommunications companies to let users know about new products and services that they could benefit from, marketers are now using it to support advertising campaigns.

Digital media

The Internet is the most well known example of digital media but other examples include CD-ROMs, DVD (Digital Video Disk), DTV (Digital Television) and Digital Radio. All, except the latter, can convey images and sounds and can be used to engage end-users, so offer vast opportunities to marketers.

The main advantage of digital media is the amount of high quality information that can be conveyed. In both b2b and b2c markets, the mailing out of CD-ROMs and mini CD-ROMs, or CD cards, which are the size of a business card and contain demonstrations and promotional material, is commonplace. The quality of image is far superior to video and it has the advantage that it can be played on a laptop, so the communication is very portable.

Digital TV offers the consumer a much greater choice of channels and some that are very specific. This means that marketers can select specific channels that are watched by their target audiences for products that do not have mass appeal. The number of new channels is increasing, as is the variety of topics, and the next development may be for large organisations to host their own TV channel!

Interactive television has become popular but not yet commonplace. This enables consumers to respond to promotions on shopping channels and engage with what is happening on screen. The advantage for marketers is that they build a database of customers who become a captive audience! This is potentially a significant step for marketing, as customers react passively to, and at arm's length with, much marketing material. Interactive television provides marketers with the opportunity to engage and interact with customers in real time.

The advantages afforded by the Internet have already been explored but it is worth noting that this medium and other digital media offer significant opportunities for marketers to build relationships with customers on an individual basis. Although this is not commonplace, it is becoming increasingly easier for organisations to identify what individual consumers are doing when they visit their web site so they know what they are interested in. This has spawned a new concept in marketing – permission marketing – as consumer protection legislation is created to enable consumers to say no to unsolicited emails.

Activity 12.3: The advantages of digital technology

Explain how digital technology is causing traditional advertisers to rethink how they communicate with customers.

Case Study – Breaking down the barriers

New technology is allowing companies to reach global customers, but communications must still be tailored to the needs of the target audience.

With pressure to centralise marketing resources, marketing departments often need to manage customer relationships across international borders and to manage these relationships remotely. What are the options facing companies looking to maintain and build on existing international customer relationships? And when is one technology approach better suited than another?

Ensuring consistency of corporate and brand identities on a global basis is a problem that has dogged marketing departments for decades. While the goal of Marketing and Brand Managers may be to communicate specific brand propositions, it's also evident that different countries have different national characteristics, languages and protocols. A marketing approach that works in one country won't necessarily work in another.

It is an issue that is particularly topical given the rapid move towards the electronic delivery of information. The use of email, fax, web and phone technologies may be ubiquitous across the Western world but that doesn't mean that the way these technologies are used by marketing departments should be the same across national borders. Cold calling, for example, is acceptable in certain countries, frowned upon in some, and banned in others.

Having said that, one cannot ignore the fact that technology is quickly making the world a smaller place and this flexibility is encouraging people to think globally. Many British companies would never have dreamed of running a marketing campaign in France a decade ago. Now, with the services of an able translator and an appropriate email list, it's possible to reach new prospects and keep existing customers informed and up to date.

In specialist global industries, this ability to reach people instantly on the other side of the world is encouraging companies to take up electronic marketing. ICIS-LOR, for example, a leading global supplier of market information to the oil and chemical industries, now uses a managed electronic broadcast service to deliver market information and reports to 3,000 customers in 94 countries in exactly the form they want, when they want it. Each customer can choose either to receive reports by post (on CD or paper), email or fax, or access reports themselves via bulletin boards, FTP sites, fax-on-demand or via the web.

Another advantage of this approach is that it is entirely automated. The systems deployed automatically send a unique selection of reports to subscribers in the media of their choice and focused monitoring and control is provided throughout the delivery process. Status reports are also provided for all traffic – an invaluable feature for determining when clients actually want to receive their report.

AMD, a major supplier of computer processors and Flash memory, also uses managed electronic broadcast services to communicate with several thousand systems integrators that are building and selling AMD processor-based systems across Europe. "We can send out an email across our marketing database within a few hours of receiving the initial templates," claims David Nelson, European reseller programme co-ordinator for AMD (UK). "If we did the same exercise by direct mail, it would not be cost-effective or time efficient. We also receive a report of undelivered emails, enabling AMD to change incorrect data in our database."

Automated email and fax broadcasting techniques are useful in cases where customers are expecting information and need to be notified on time, every time. When a more personal touch is required, such as in cases where companies are trying to qualify sales leads, the phone is often the preferred option.

Operating cross-border telemarketing campaigns, however, is invariably a lot more complex than undertaking cross-border electronic broadcasting campaigns. To begin with, people implementing campaigns need to be fluent in the language of the country they are calling and that often means hiring specialist staff. Local legislation must also be looked at to ensure no local laws are going to be broken. And then there is the simple fact that the way business is conducted in different countries can be quite different. Knowing the right way to approach a campaign is often just a question of experience.

"It's very important to respect local laws and customs", says Gary Slade, Sales Director at Sitel Corporation, a provider of outsourced telemarketing and CRM services. "But that doesn't mean you necessarily need to employ local people to run campaigns. It's often much more cost-effective to operate from a single site with centralised resources than to try and operate several international operations."

Sitel operates from 77 customer contact centres in 19 countries and offers services in more than 25 languages. "We can initiate calls locally or from the UK – it really isn't a big issue," says Slade. "Although phone bills are lower if you're calling locally, as we have a full European footprint with offices connected to a Virtual Private Network, the cost of making international calls can be relatively low. If we had, say, ten people doing a programme in Germany, I wouldn't be surprised if the cost of a flight from the UK and single overnight hotel stay to oversee the campaign didn't offset any advantage gained from the lower local call costs."

Establishing rules of engagement for outbound calling campaigns is another challenge. Slade observes: "While not every country has a formal Telephone Preference Service (TPS) or Fax Preference Service (FPS) where consumers can register their name to opt out of 'cold calling/faxing' campaigns, every country has regulations. Germany, for example, is very strong on privacy laws. Companies must have an existing relationship and have the customer's permission to be able to make calls. This makes outbound cold calling difficult but not impossible – you just need to find a way to address these issues and still meet a company's objectives."

Such artificial barriers go to prove Slade's point that an important aspect of running a successful country-specific campaign is to take note of that country's requirements. "You can never just lift a programme from one country and put it in another," says Slade. "You must first translate its language and style. Our approach is to plan globally but implement locally." Sitel has used this experience to build a suite of 'frameworks' that looks at different delivery options. These frameworks take into account what the client is trying to achieve and any country-specific relevant factors. "It's rather like hanging clothes on a mannikin," says Slade. "We can look at factors such as: When do I call? Who are realistic targets? Should it be a free trial? And for inbound calling activity, what tariff (0800, national, premium rate etc.) should be used?"

When it comes to conducting telephone-based marketing campaigns, recruiting the right people is key. "There's no point in recruiting customer care people for marketing campaigns. You need to recruit the right people and then invest in training them using the local language materials. If you have the right people, the level of training required is relatively even across all countries."

Interestingly though, Sitel is not a great exponent of using home-based telemarketing workers. "We have looked into it many times but are not convinced it works effectively. How, for example, can you maintain quality and training levels when people are not in the same office – or even in the same country? And how do you conduct technical support on agents' machines? It's just not something we're comfortable to deploy widely at this stage."

In an age where companies are being told that to survive and prosper they must deliver information to customers when they want it and how they want it, a mixed media approach may be the best way forward.

On occasions, this will mean using traditional direct marketing techniques backed up by outbound or inbound telemarketing. On others, it may well mean using automated email or fax broadcasts backed up by telemarketing, or a combination of all options.

In terms of which media is most appropriate to which country, again there are no hard and fast rules. The US and Scandinavian countries are generally perceived to prefer email, while countries like Italy and Turkey are keener on voice communications. The UK is perhaps in the middle. However, there are such marked differences between industry sectors within countries that it's difficult to draw many conclusions from this.

Automated email and fax options are cost-effective for both inbound and outbound activities but are not always appropriate, which is why the telemarketing industry continues to flourish. So long as providers of email, fax and telemarketing campaigns are honest about the merits of their respective trades, there is no reason for a conflict of interests. Providers need each other to provide their customers with a complete service.

Source: *Marketing Business,* December/January 2002.

Questions

1. What are the main advantages of electronic communications over direct mail for AMD?
2. What are the implications for marketers operating international campaigns compared to their native country?

SUMMARY OF KEY POINTS

- ICT has enlarged the opportunities that marketers have to communicate and interact with different stakeholder groups.
- New communication channels and media include email, WAP, Internet and digital TV and radio.
- New media has increased the opportunities for marketers to target individuals with personalised messages.

Improving and developing own learning

The following projects are designed to help you to develop your knowledge and skills further by carrying out some research yourself. Feedback is not provided for this type of learning because there are no 'answers' to be found, but you may wish to discuss your findings with colleagues and fellow students.

Project A

Contact Managers within your organisation, or one you know well, to discuss the way new media are used in the organisation to communicate with internal and external customers.

Project B

Imagine that you are a Sales Manager with a team of salespeople in the field who have recently been issued with laptops.

List the communication and management uses for this equipment.

Project C

You are developing an online shopping facility for a large retail organisation.

List the features that you would include to enable the organisation to interact effectively with its customers.

Feedback on activities

Activity 12.1: Internet benefits

Dimension	Advantages
Speed.	■ Information is available immediately to consumers who have Internet access. ■ A 'contact us' button or similar means that individual questions from consumers can be individually and promptly answered.
Convenience for consumers.	■ Consumers can access web sites at a time that is suitable for them. Therefore advertising and promotional messages are available at a time that is convenient for the consumer, and not slotted into a favourite TV programme for example.
Currency.	■ Company web sites can be updated on a regular basis, so catalogues can be kept up to date cost-effectively. ■ Information can be posted almost as soon as it happens – useful in a crisis situation.
Interactivity.	■ Two-way communication is possible. ■ Consumers can take part in online discussions with television celebrities. ■ Opportunity to build customer and client relationships.
Direct communication.	■ Direct mail companies use the Internet to target their promotions to specific audiences or individuals.

Cost-effectiveness.	■ A wider audience of consumers can be reached. ■ Individual targeting is possible. ■ Administration costs are reduced compared to other communication systems.
Customer feedback.	■ Feedback can be gathered from individual customers cost-effectively.

Activity 12.2: Poppy site success

ICT was used in the following ways:

- Cold emailing.
- Emailing current supporters.
- Promotions on key search engines.
- Informative web site providing opportunity for donations.

Activity 12.3: The advantages of digital technology

You may have thought of all or some of the following:

- Customers using direct response television, which is connected to a telephone line, can shop online by pressing a button on their special remote control sets. When an advertisement triggers desire they can immediately connect to the organisation selling the product. Advertisers are now dealing with people who can respond immediately, so the message needs to take them through 'AIDA' rather than simply inform.
- The Internet is a very versatile medium for advertisers to raise awareness of the range of products, key benefits, and USPs. In contrast to other creative media such as television and cinema, the consumer can access at own convenience.
- Email enables advertisers to target consumers with offers and information individually. However, best practice demands that consumers need to be given the opportunity to unsubscribe.
- Advertisers now have the opportunity to send text messages to mobile phone users – again the problem of consumer annoyance to unsolicited messages must be borne in mind.

Glossary

Glossary

The following relevant terms have been taken from the CIM's online glossary. If you would like to see a full listing of marketing terms please visit www.cim.co.uk, and look under Services and then the Library and Information Service section of the site.

Above-the-line – advertising for which a payment is made and for which a commission is paid to the advertising agency.

Account management – the process by which an agency or supplier manages the needs of a client.

ACORN – a classification of residential neighbourhoods – a database which divides up the entire population of the UK in terms of housing in which they live.

Added value – the increase in worth of a product or service as a result of a particular activity – in the context of marketing this might be packaging or branding.

Advertising – promotion of a product, service or message by an identified sponsor using paid for media.

AIDA – attention, interest, desire, action – a model describing the process that advertising or promotion is intended to initiate in the mind of a prospective customer.

Ansoff matrix – model relating marketing strategy to general strategic direction. It maps product/market strategies.

BCG matrix – model for product portfolio analysis.

Below-the-line – non-media advertising or promotion when no commission has been paid to the advertising agency.

Brand – the set of physical attributes of a product or service, together with the beliefs and expectations surrounding it.

Business plan – a strategic document showing cash flow, forecasts and direction of a company.

Business strategy – the means by which a business works towards achieving its stated aims.

Business to business (b2b) – relating to the sale of a product for any use other than personal consumption.

Business to consumer (b2c) – relating to the sale of a product for personal consumption.

Buying behaviour – the process that buyers go through when deciding whether or not to purchase goods or services.

Channels – the methods used by a company to communicate and interact with its customers.

Comparative advertising – advertising which compares a company's product with that of competing brands.

Competitive advantage – the product, proposition or benefit that puts a company ahead of its competitors.

Confusion marketing – controversial strategy of deliberately confusing the customer.

Consumer – individual who buys and uses a product or service.

Consumer behaviour – the buying habits and patterns of consumers in the acquisition and usage of products and services.

Copyright – the law that protects the originator's material from unauthorised use, usually (in the UK) for seventy years after the originator's death.

Corporate identity – the character a company seeks to establish for itself in the mind of the public.

Corporate reputation – a complex mix of characteristics such as ethos, identity and image that go to make up a company's public personality.

Culture – a shared set of values, beliefs and traditions that influence prevailing behaviour within a country or organisation.

Customer – a person or company who purchases goods or services.

Customer loyalty – feelings or attitudes that incline a customer to return to a company, shop or outlet to purchase there again.

Customer Relationship Management (CRM) – the coherent management of contacts and interactions with customers.

Customer satisfaction – the provision of goods or services which fulfil the customer's expectations in terms of quality and service, in relation to price paid.

DAGMAR – defining advertising goals for measured advertising response – a model for planning advertising in such a way that its success can be quantitatively monitored.

Data processing – the obtaining, recording and holding of information which can then be retrieved, used, disseminated or erased.

Data Protection Act – a law which makes organisations responsible for protecting the privacy of personal data.

Database marketing – whereby customer information stored in an electronic database is utilised for targeting marketing activities.

Decision Making Unit (DMU) – the team of people in an organisation or family group who make the final buying decision.

Demographic data – information describing and segmenting a population in terms of age, sex, income and so on which can be used to target marketing campaigns.

Differentiation – ensuring that products and services have a unique element to allow them to stand out from the rest.

Direct mail – delivery of an advertising or promotional message to customers or potential customers by mail.

Direct marketing – all activities that make it possible to offer goods or services or to transmit other messages to a segment of the population by post, telephone, email or other direct means.

Direct response advertising – advertising incorporating a contact method such as a phone number or enquiry form with the intention of encouraging the recipient to respond directly to the advertiser.

Distribution (place) – the process of getting the goods from the manufacturer or supplier to the user.

Diversification – an increase in the variety of goods and services produced by an organisation.

E-commerce – business conducted electronically.

E-marketing – marketing conducted electronically.

Electronic Point of Sale (EPOS) – a system whereby electronic tills are used to process customer transactions in a retail outlet.

Ethical marketing – marketing that takes account of the moral aspects of decisions.

Export marketing – the marketing of goods or services to overseas customers.

Field marketing – extending an organisation's marketing in the field through merchandising, product launches, training of retail staff, etc.

FMCG – fast-moving consumer goods, such as packages of food and toiletries.

Focus groups – a tool for marketing research where small groups of participants take part in guided discussions on the topic being researched.

Forecasting – calculation of future events and performance.

Franchising – the selling of a licence by the owner (franchisor) to a third party (franchisee) permitting the sale of a product or service for a specified period.

Geo-demographics – a method of analysis combining geographic and demographic variables.

Grey market (or silver market) – term used to define a population over a certain age (usually 65).

Industrial marketing (or business to business marketing) – the marketing of industrial products.

Innovation – development of new products, services or ways of working.

Internal customers – employees within an organisation viewed as 'consumers' of a product or service provided by another part of the organisation.

Internal marketing – the process of eliciting support for a company and its activities among its own employees in order to encourage them to promote its goals.

International marketing – the conduct and co-ordination of marketing activities in more than one country.

Key account management – account management as applied to a company's most valuable customers.

Logo – a graphic usually consisting of a symbol and or group of letters that identifies a company or brand.

Macro environment – the external factors which affect companies' planning and performance, and are beyond its control. (SLEPT).

Market development – the process of growing sales by offering existing products (or new versions of them) to new customer groups.

Market penetration – the attempt to grow one's business by obtaining a larger market share in an existing market.

Market research – the gathering and analysis of data relating to markets to inform decision making.

Marketing research – the gathering and analysis of data relating to marketing to inform decision making (includes product research, place research, pricing research, etc.).

Market segmentation – the division of the marketplace into distinct sub-groups or segments, each characterised by particular tastes and requiring a specific marketing mix.

Market share – a company's sales of a given product or set of products to a given set of customers expressed as a percentage of total sales of all such products to such customers.

Marketing audit – scrutiny of an organisation's existing marketing system to ascertain its strengths and weaknesses.

Marketing communications (promotion) – all methods used by a firm to communicate with its customers and stakeholders.

Marketing information – any information used or required to support marketing decisions.

Marketing mix – the combination of marketing inputs that affect customer motivation and behaviour (7Ps – product, price, promotion, place, people, process and physical evidence).

Marketing orientation – a business strategy whereby customers' needs and wants determine corporate direction.

Marketing planning – the selection and scheduling of activities to support the company's chosen marketing strategy or goals.

Marketing strategy – the broad methods chosen to achieve marketing objectives.

Micro environment – the immediate context of a company's operations, including such elements as suppliers, customers and competitors.

Mission statement – a company's summary of business philosophy, purpose and direction.

Model – simplified representation of a process, designed to aid in understanding.

New Product Development (NPD) – the creation of new products from evaluation of proposals through to launch.

Niche marketing – the marketing of a product to a small and well-defined segment of the marketplace.

Objectives – a company's defined and measurable aims or goals for a given period.

Packaging – material used to protect and promote goods.

Personal selling – one-to-one communication between seller and prospective purchaser.

PIMS – profit impact of marketing strategies – A US database supplying data such as environment, strategy, competition and internal data.

Porter's five forces – an analytic model developed by Michael E. Porter which analyses the competitive environment and industry structure.

Positioning – the creation of an image for a product or service in the minds of customers, both specifically to that item and in relation to competitive offerings.

Product life cycle – a model describing the progress of a product from the inception of the idea through the peak of sales, to its decline.

Promotional mix – the components of an individual campaign which are likely to include advertising, personal selling, public relations, direct marketing, packaging and sales promotion.

Public Relations (PR) – the planned and sustained communication to promote mutual understanding between an organisation and its stakeholders.

Pull promotion – addresses the customer directly with a view to getting them to demand the product and hence 'pull' it down through the distribution chain.

Push promotion – relies on the next link in the distribution chain, e.g. wholesaler, to 'push' out products to the customer.

Qualitative research – information that cannot be measured or expressed in numeric terms. It is useful to the marketer as it often explores people's feelings and opinions.

Quantitative research – information that can be measured in numeric terms and analysed statistically.

Reference group – a group with which the customer identifies in some way and whose opinions and experiences influence the customer's behaviour.

Relationship marketing – the strategy of establishing a relationship with a customer which continues well beyond the first purchase.

Return on investment – the value that an organisation derives from investing in a project.

Sales promotion – a range of techniques used to increase sales in the short term.

Skimming – setting the original price high in the early stages of the product life cycle to get as much profit as possible before prices are driven down by increasing competition.

SLEPT – a framework for viewing the macro environment – socio-cultural, legal, economic, political and technical factors.

SMART – a mnemonic referring to the need for objectives to be specific, measurable, achievable, relevant and timebound.

Sponsorship – specialised form of promotion where a company will help fund an event or support a business venture in return for publicity.

Stakeholder – an individual or group that affects or is affected by the organisation and its operations.

Supplier – an organisation or individual that supplies goods or services to a company.

Targeting – the use of market segmentation to select and address a key group of potential purchasers.

Unique Selling Proposition (USP) – the benefit that a product or service can deliver to customers that is not offered by any competitor.

Vision – the long term aims and aspirations of the company for itself.

Word of mouth – the spreading of information through human interaction alone.

Appendix 1

Feedback to Case Studies

Session 1 – PC World

1. What evidence is there in the Case Study that PC World are focused on the needs of their customers?

   - Awareness of customer characteristics – non-techies etc.
   - Commitment to improving after-sales service.
   - Desire to build ongoing relationship.

2. What suggestions can you make to help PC World identify the future needs of their customers?

   - Customer surveys via telephone, mail or email.
   - Feedback from engineers and staff operating after-sales services.
   - Feedback from front-line staff working in the retail outlets.

3. What benefits do they expect to gain from introducing First Call?

   - Reducing the number of calls from frustrated buyers who do not understand how to set up their new PC.
   - Opportunity to cross-sell other products.
   - Ability to generate greater loyalty.
   - Satisfied customers!

Session 2 – I want a relationship

1. What examples can you find in the Case Study that indicates that many organisations are not very skilled at building effective relationships with customers?

   - Lack of understanding about type of data that is really required – just build a database and hope for the best.
   - Purchase CRM systems without trying them out for what the organisation wants – do they know in the first place?
   - Do not keep the database up to date.

2. What advice does James Wilson give to prospective purchasers of CRM systems?

   - Identify what you need it to do for you and then try it out before you buy.

3. Why do you think that Duncan Painter describes CRM as a cultural change as much as a technology change?

   - Because it is as much a 'way of life' within the organisation as an activity using the appropriate technology.
   - People's behaviour within the organisation must reflect the desire to understand each customer (internal and external) and how they can meet their needs.

Session 3 – The UK car industry

REPORT

Subject: Key changes in the UK car sales market
Author: Kay Ling, Marketing Assistant
FAO: T. Hirji, marketing Manager
Date: 17 June 200X

1. Introduction

This report seeks to highlight key changes affecting the car sales market following the report into high car prices in the UK published by the Competition Commission.

2. Methodology

The information has been gathered from information reported in the trade press and the Internet.

3. Findings

3.1 Traditional car sales market

Dealers buy from main manufacturers and advertise cars at official list price, leading to limited price competition.

Private buyers buy through the network of franchised dealers.

Strong brand loyalty and a relatively stable structure in the UK market with few buyers looking to purchase outside the UK.

3.2 Changes to the traditional car sales market

The recently published report by the Competition Commission has highlighted the fact that UK car prices are high and more expensive than elsewhere. Car makers and importers will no longer have direct control of prices resulting in greater competition. The growth of the single market mentality has forced prices down.

Car makers and importers have lost control over supply channels as dealers are now able to obtain cars from cheaper sources in Europe.

UK motorists realise that the franchise dealers are not the only places to buy new cars especially as they are more expensive. UK motorists are now more prepared to shop around and are aware of cheaper sources such as mainland Europe, the Internet and car supermarkets. Speculation suggests that unofficial imports will rise to 110,000, which represents more than 10% of the UK market.

Car supermarkets are perceived to be the cheapest way to buy cars in the UK according to a recent survey by *What Car* magazine. They are seen as promoting a friendly, non-pressurised environment for buyers.

One growth sector of the retail motor trade are cyber-dealers such as Direct Line's jamjar.com, virgincars.com and oneswoop.com. It is likely that there will be other new entrants in the form of Sainbury's and Tesco supermarkets.

Growth in the car sales market has been limited, possibly due to anticipation of the Commission's report.

It is predicted by Cap Gemini that in the next three years dealers will account for only 60% of car sales, cyber-dealers for 15% and car supermarkets for 25%.

Conclusions

There is change in the traditional market and that looks set to accelerate as UK motorists continue to shop around for cheaper prices. The publication of the report by the Competition Commission has stimulated this.

Consumers face real choice for the first time in the UK market and this looks as if it will continue to increase. The level of imports from Europe is set to rise and should be closely monitored to measure the impact on car supermarket sales.

Car supermarkets are currently well positioned in this price-sensitive market to attract buyers' attention and capture sales.

Recommendations

The changes happening in the car sales market are monitored closely over the next twelve months as reaction to the report by the Competition Commission continues to grow.

If price is a major factor influencing purchase then car supermarkets, like Jacey Motors, should build on their existing reputation.

As competition in this sector will probably increase, Jacey Motors should identify a USP and look for ways to differentiate themselves from the competition.

If the Internet is set to grow as a car sales distribution channel then Jacey Motors should also consider online selling.

Session 4 – Cooper's Edinburgh office

As Manager of the Edinburgh office you have been asked to prepare a report of the first year's performance to present at the next meeting of Partners.

Prepare slides to support your presentation on client list and number of cases per client, the number of new cases coming into the office month by month and fees earned by staff.

Cases per Client

Commercial Insurance	89	44%
NIB Insurance	70	34%
Perfect Homebuilders	20	10%
PBC Construction	9	4%
Econ	6	3%
Rosso Wines	5	2%
Medcare	2	1%
Jenkins & Co	1	1%
Pemberton & Sons	1	1%
TOTAL	**203**	**100%**

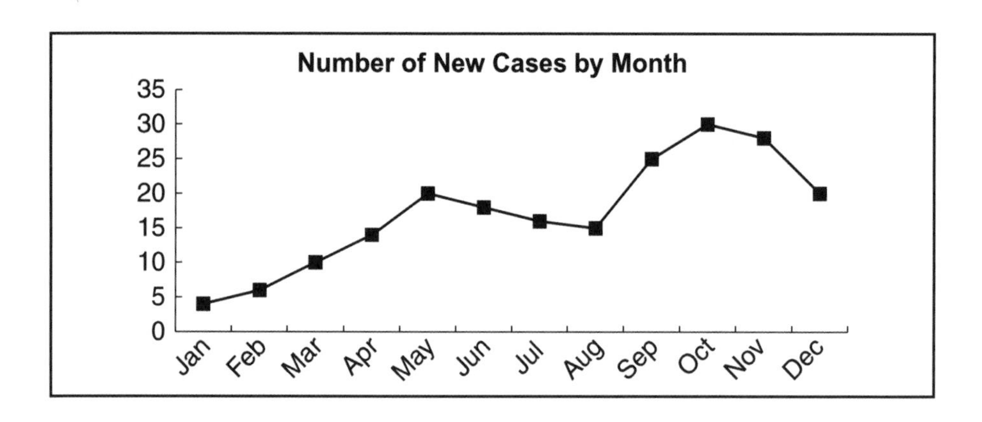

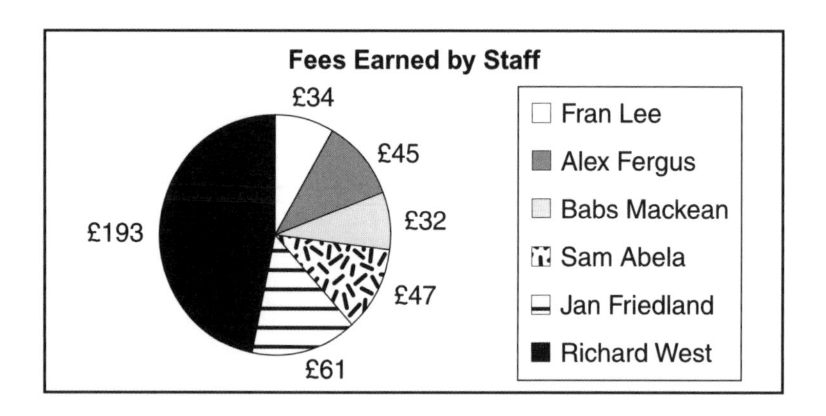

Session 5 – Customer service in decline

1. What are the benefits for organisations of measuring levels of customer service?

   - If you don't measure it is difficult to control or improve. Measuring gives an indication of 'where you are now' as a base for moving forward.
   - Measuring progress means that organisations can identify the size and nature of improvements which can be used in communications to internal and external staff.
   - They are able to benchmark against the norms for industry or competitors if the information is available.

2. What are the disadvantages of the short-term strategies employed by the telecommunications industry?

   - Looking for short-term benefits rather than building customer relationships.
   - May prevent development of customer loyalty.
   - Prevents the industry from looking at what is wrong – emphasis is on promotion.

3. What evidence can you find in the Case Study to suggest that training in customer service skills is important in the organisation's ability to offer quality service?

   - Increasing customer demands making it essential for organisations to have knowledgeable and skilled staff.
   - The length of time taken to train skills.
   - Customers appear to prefer human contact.

Session 6 – Evolving the supply chain

1. What are the advantages that manufacturers are hoping to gain from building a support chain?
   - USP.
   - Continued relationship.
   - Additional revenue.
   - Competitive advantage.
2. How can they communicate this to customers?
   - Personal selling.
   - Brochure.
   - Trade shows.
   - Advertising.
   - Company web site.
   - PR such as articles in trade journals and professional magazines read by target audience.

Session 7 – Marketing magic

1. What promotional tools have been used by Bloomsbury to market Harry?
   - PR, press advertising, outdoor advertising, merchandising/point of sale.
2. What unusual activities and events took place?
   - Slumber parties.
   - Steam train – Hogwarts Express – publicity tour.
   - July launch – normally avoided by publishers.
   - Timing of launch – 3.45pm.
3. How did Bloomsbury take advantage of the adult market?
   - Re-jacketing the books so adults could be seen reading them!
   - Important factor was maintaining brand recognition.

Session 8 – Disaster moves

1. What was the difference in the response to crisis by P&O and Coca-Cola in the Case Study and what were the results?

    - P&O acted immediately and decisively with recompense for disappointed passengers with the result that most were sympathetic to P&O. They spoke for P&O to the media, not against them.
    - Coca-Cola delayed so had control of the situation taken out of their hands. The result was bad publicity, a ban on product sales in several countries and destruction of Belgian imports in the Netherlands.

2. What are the potential costs of crisis?

    - Loss of market share.
    - Reduction in share prices.
    - Loss of sales.
    - Product ban.
    - Loss of good reputation.
    - Adverse publicity.
    - Low staff morale.

3. Why is it good advice to tell it all and tell it quick?

    - If you don't, someone else will – and not in the way you would. They may have a 'hidden agenda' or be ill-informed.
    - Bad news is news, so journalists may not give a balanced story if not given a prepared statement.
    - Staff will hear it from you not the media.
    - You maintain control of the situation.

Session 9 – Consumer turn-off for TV ads

Internal memorandum

To: F. Fielder, Marketing Manager
From: H. Dibner, Marketing Executive
Date: 23 March 200X

Subject: Findings from survey published by CIA Sensor on consumers perceptions on current levels of advertising

1. Introduction

This survey represents consumers' evaluations of the amount of advertising that they are exposed to and their attitude towards radio, print and TV advertising. Consumers from nine European countries and the US were included in the survey and this brief report highlights some of the main points reported in *Marketing Business* about the findings of this survey.

2. Findings

2.1 General

More people claim to avoid ads related to buying than are inspired by them. The nature of the ad medium has affects the degree of ad annoyance and there are variations across different countries. Of the ten markets surveyed, the UK had the second lowest level of ad avoidance.

2.2 TV advertising

Although TV ads are found to be more engaging, ads are found to be more intrusive.

Generally TV ads provide less inspiration than annoyance, except in the UK, Ireland and Italy.

In the case of TV, an average of 45% across all countries try to avoid the ads with the figures being highest in Italy (76%) and Spain (69%) where TV advertising is heaviest. Italians view around 700 ads per week while the Spaniards see over 600.

CIA suggests shorter but more frequent ad breaks might be a way around the avoidance factor.

TV advertising comes out top as the best source of inspiration for purchases. In countries where Internet penetration is high – UK, Germany and USA – it is also regarded as a good source of shopping ideas.

2.3 Print advertising

Although TV advertising comes out top as the best source of inspiration for purchases, print advertising follows closely behind.

Magazines and newspapers provide more inspiration to buy than annoyance.

When print ads match content, readers tend to perceive a relevant message in the ads and are, therefore, less likely to regard them negatively.

2.4 Radio advertising

Radio ads are seen as less intrusive when the radio is being played as a background to an activity.

3. Conclusions

Results vary across the ten countries as might be expected but generally, TV ads are found to cause significant annoyance compared to ads in other media.

However, TV advertising is engaging, being a creative medium, and the CIA suggest that shorter, more frequent breaks might be a way of reducing the annoyance factor.

Print ads appear to provide more inspiration to buy than TV in most countries.

Recommendations

To continue with TV advertising but be more aware of the avoidance factor. Look for ways of reducing this.

Consider greater use of print advertising as this provides greater inspiration to buy.

Session 10 – Bulletin PR

1. What lessons can you learn from the information in the Case Study about successful PR at exhibitions?

   - Speed of communication is important to be ahead of competitors.
   - Accurate targeting significantly improves results.
   - The importance of cultural differences when planning how to communicate.

2. What does Hayward think are the relative merits of advertising and PR in terms of communication?

   - Advertising guarantees exposure.
   - PR has credibility to back it up.

3. How were the results of the Lotus exhibition measured?

   - Measurement of correct understanding of message (69% of comment).
   - Share of voice in show coverage (10%).
   - Confirmed orders.
   - Quality leads.

Session 11 – Tyres: the branding challenge

1. What does Betes think is important for consumers to feel when offered a brand of tyre by fitters?

   - Confidence in the brand.
   - Recognition of the brand – familiarity.

2. How is the Conti brand communicated to consumers?

   - Previously sponsorship.
   - Currently TV and press advertising in Europe adapting concepts according to language and culture.

3. What are the barriers faced by Betes to creating brand awareness and developing brand loyalty?

   - Communicating through tyre fitters.
   - Dull image of product.
   - Dealers' lack of pro-activity or awareness of the need for product promotion.

Session 12 – Breaking down the barriers

1. What are the main advantages of electronic communications over direct mail for AMD?

   - Time efficiency.
   - Reduced costs.
   - Report on undelivered emails enables AMD to amend their database.

2. What are the implications for marketers operating international campaigns compared to working in their native country?

   - Language barrier.
   - Observing local customs.
   - Different ways of doing business.

Appendix 2

Syllabus

Customer Communications

Aim

The Customer Communications module provides the entry level skills and application in the development and use of communications for Stage 1. It aims to provide participants with a working knowledge of customers' buying behaviour and the promotional mix as well as communications techniques.

Participants will not be expected to have any prior qualifications or experience in a marketing role. They will be expected to be conversant with the content of the Marketing Fundamentals module before undertaking this module.

Related statements of practice

Cb.1 Develop direct or indirect communications.

Cb.2 Deliver direct or indirect communications.

Gb.1 Support the management of customer relationships.

Gb.2 Deliver effective customer service.

Learning outcomes

Participants will be able to:

- Recognise organisations as open systems and explain the importance of relationships between the organisation and its suppliers, intermediaries, customers and other key stakeholders in a changing environment.
- Explain why it is important for marketers to understand consumer and industrial buying behaviour for marketing decisions.
- Explain the elements of the promotional mix and its fit with the marketing planning process.
- Explain the advantages and disadvantages of the range of communications tools available to an organisation.
- Develop internal and external communications using appropriate tools to suit a variety of target audiences and using an understanding of customer behaviour and customer information.

- Select appropriate verbal and non-verbal communications with people inside and outside the organisation.
- Demonstrate the importance of customers and customer service and apply customer care principles to create positive relationships with customers in a variety of contexts.

Knowledge and skill requirements

Element 1: Customers and stakeholders (20%)

1.1 Explain what is meant by the terms 'customer', 'stakeholder' and 'user'.

1.2 Demonstrate the fundamental importance of 'customers' to all forms of organisations, including services and the need to clearly identify them.

1.3 Describe the link between the marketing concept, a customer focus and relationship marketing.

1.4 Appreciate the need for effective internal and external customer communications and their link to and role in maintaining customer focus, developing and sustaining good customer relations and relationship marketing in creating loyalty and customer retention.

1.5 List the factors that cause change in customers and the subsequent impact on marketing programmes.

Element 2: Buying behaviour (10%)

2.1 Explain the difference between consumer buyer behaviour and organisational buyer behaviour.

2.2 Explain the importance of understanding buyer behaviour.

2.3 Describe the Decision Making Unit (DMU) and the roles of its constituents.

2.4 The Decision Making Process (DMP) for consumers and organisations.

2.5 The impact and effect of the DMU and the DMP on the communications mix.

Element 3: Implementing elements of the promotional mix (50%)

3.1 Explain the concept of, and need for, an integrated marketing communications approach and the links between communications and marketing planning.

3.2 Explain the role and importance of promotion in marketing.

3.3 Explain the structure and function of the communication process.

3.4 Describe the tools of promotion (the promotion mix).

3.5 Explain the planning process for developing and implementing promotional strategies and individual elements of the promotional mix.

3.6 Explain how above-the-line and below-the-line activities are used.

3.7 Explain the key stages and considerations when developing and designing advertisements.

3.8 Describe the role and scope of PR and its contribution to the promotional mix.

3.9 Explain the role of corporate identity, brand image and logos in corporate communication with customers.

3.10 Distinguish between the different forms of integrated mail media, such as direct mail leaflets and mail order advertising.

3.11 Explain the role of Point of Sale (POS) material and how it is developing in response to changing customer needs.

3.12 Explain the role of packaging in the promotions mix.

3.13 Describe the role of exhibitions as a communications tool and their role in promotions.

3.14 Explain the role of Information and Communications Technology (ICT) in communications, including digital TV and interactive marketing.

3.15 Describe current trends and developments in promotions and their impact on organisations.

Element 4: Face to face communication (10%)

4.1 Describe the communication process and explain the importance and the advantages and disadvantages of different types of communication in a variety of face to face situations.

4.2 Identify barriers to communication and explain how they can be avoided and overcome.

4.3 Explain the communications planning process to produce effective strategies for improving alternative communications formats.

4.4 Explain the importance of effective body language, tone, verbal and listening skills in communication and strategies for developing and improving verbal, non-verbal and listening skills.

4.5 Interpret, summarise and present oral, written and graphical information.

4.6 Explain key communication factors to consider in meetings, including arranging and convening a meeting, documentation involved and strategies for conducting a meeting.

4.7 Plan, prepare and deliver a presentation using appropriate and effective visual aids and media.

4.8 Use a variety of formats to communicate with internal and external customers including telephone, letters, memoranda, notices, reports and emails.

Element 5: Customer service and customer care (10%)

5.1 Explain the concept of customer care and its importance in consumer, business to business, not-for-profit and public sector organisations.

5.2 Explain the importance of quality and customer care and methods of achieving quality.

5.3 Explain the relationship between customer care, customer focus and relationship marketing.

5.4 Explain the importance of obtaining customer feedback and devising contingencies for dealing with customer complaints.

5.5 Describe how to plan and establish a customer care programme.

5.6 Demonstrate an understanding of how ICT is used in customer service, for example through the use of databases.

Appendix 3

Specimen examination paper

Certificate in Marketing

Customer Communications

5.20: Customer Communications

Time:

Date:

3 Hours Duration

This examination is in two sections.

PART A – Is compulsory and worth 40% of total marks.

PART B – Has **SIX** questions; select **THREE**. Each answer will be worth 20% of the total marks.

DO NOT repeat the question in your answer, but show clearly the number of the question attempted on the appropriate pages of the answer book.

Rough workings should be included in the answer book and ruled through after use.

Certificate in Marketing

5.20: Customer Communications – Specimen Paper

PART A

The UK Small Car Market

There is not much to choose between one small car and another in today's market. They are all reliable, offer similar equipment and are similarly priced within their ranges. Yet car manufacturers spent over £120 million on advertising in 1997 to persuade customers that there really is a difference between models such as the Ford Fiesta, Vauxhall Corsa and Nissan Micra.

Advertising plays a crucial role in brand and model choice by building image and promoting real and apparent differences in price and finance. Getting the right image for a model is important but manufacturers also need to carefully target their potential customers using direct marketing techniques.

Based on research undertaken by Lifestyle Research during 1998, car advertisements appear to have more impact on men than women. Men tend to have better recall for the less prominent models. The skew is particularly marked for BMW and Daewoo, men being nearly three times more likely than women to remember these advertisements.

ABC1 drivers are more conscious of car advertising than those in the C2DE social grade groups, perhaps because the first group are twice as likely to be driving new as opposed to second-hand cars. Of the various models with the highest recall levels, only Ford, Nissan and Vauxhall have higher recall levels among C2DE drivers.

Twenty seven per cent of drivers remember receiving a direct mailshot promoting a car during the previous month. For company and new car drivers, this figure rose to 37%.

In the lifestyle research survey, all respondents were asked about activities undertaken in the past six months: 30% had watched a specialist car programme on television; 25% had visited a car dealer; 8% had taken a test drive and 5% had requested a brochure.

Television and newspaper advertising were used extensively, demonstrating that mass media advertising is considered essential to compete effectively in the market, even though the number of buyers in any one year is very small compared with most markets.

A large proportion of Fiestas, the UK's most popular models, are either second-hand cars or form part of company fleets.

Figure 1.

Recall of Advertising in Past Month (% Drivers)	
Nissan	33
Vauxhall	38
Rover	17
Ford	44
Renault	27

Source: Car Market, July 1998

Figure 2.

Media Considered to be Informative (% Drivers Intending to Buy New Cars)	
Local press advertisements	40
National press advertisements	27
TV advertisements	18
Direct mailshots	11
Radio	4

Source: Car Market, October 1998

Figure 3.

Top Six Selling Small Cars – 1997						
Model	Rover 200	Renault Clio	Vauxhall Corsa	Peugeot 306	Nissan Micra	Ford Fiesta
Cars sold	40,000	60,000	80,000	50,000	38,000	125,000

Source: Car Market, March 1998

Figure 4.

Car Ownership Per Home of those Owning at Least One Car – Number Owned by Age of Head of Household				
Cars Per Home	All Homes	Head of Household Aged <45	Head of Household Aged 45-64	Head of Household Aged >65
One	70%	65%	58%	80%
Two	25%	30%	30%	18%
Three	5%	5%	12%	2%

Source: Car Market, May 1998

Figure 5.

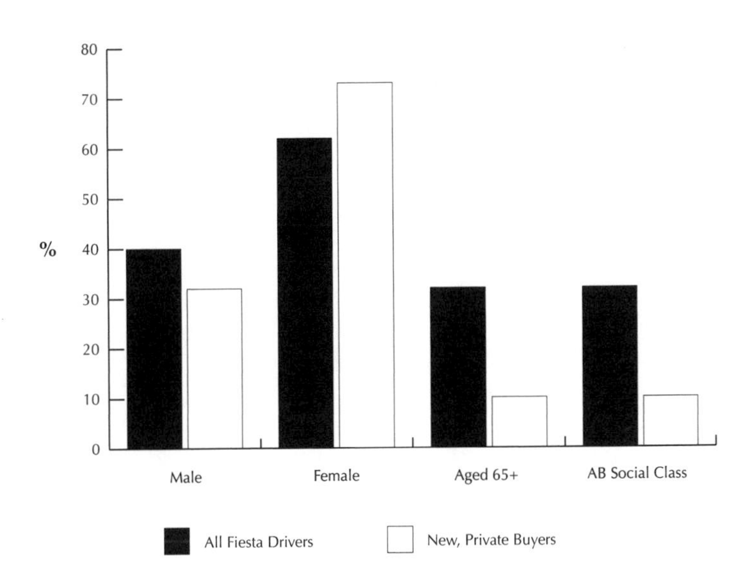

Source: Lifestyle Data, 1998

PART A

Question 1.

As Product Manager for the Ford Fiesta, you are responsible for analysing key data printed in articles in the consumer and trade press. You have extracted the above information from various articles in *Car Market,* the industry's trade paper.

a. In a formal report format addressed to the Marketing Manager for Ford (UK), analyse the data provided and provide reasoned recommendations for how the Fiesta should be marketed in the future. Be selective with the data as appropriate to the case presented in your report.

(25 marks)

b. Add three appendices to your report which should include the following:

i) A line graph to show recall of advertising in the past month.

ii) A component bar chart to show the number of cars owned per home.

iii) A pie chart to show the market share of the top six selling small cars.

(15 marks)
(40 marks in total)

PART B – Answer THREE Questions Only

Question 2.

Your company has recently appointed a new Product Manager to your team who has very little experience in delivering presentations at meetings. To assist your new team member, do the following:

a. Draft an agenda, where one item of business is a presentation from the Product Manager.

(10 marks)

b. Write a memorandum on how to make an effective presentation.

(10 marks)
(20 marks in total)

Question 3.

You work as a Sponsorship Assistant for a local dog rescue home. Draft a letter to a large petroleum company asking for corporate sponsorship for a newsletter that you send to regular contributors. You will need to provide some information about the newsletter in terms of its content, distribution and details about its target audience. You should indicate the amount of sponsorship that is required. Your letter should also explain the potential benefits to the sponsor in communicating with this target audience.

(20 marks)

Question 4.

You work as a Marketing Manager for a large toy manufacturer and you are about to launch a new range of toys aimed at children under 5 years of age. Draft a full A4 page recruitment advertisement for the post of Product Manager for this toy range to be placed in *Marketing Recruitment.* Ensure the advertisement contains the following: the company background; the benefits of the job; information about the role; a brief description of the ideal candidate and any other essential information. Provide guidance for the magazine's production department with regards to the typeface and type sizes to be used, the positioning of logos and any other layout details you consider necessary.

(20 marks)

Question 5.

As Customer Care Manager for a company of your choice, you regularly conduct research on the levels of customer complaints, particularly with regards to the telephone manner of your operatives in your Call Centre. Your recent research highlights an alarming increase in the levels of customer complaints, so you feel the time has come to instigate a new, improved Customer Care Programme. Draft an email to your Line Manager outlining the following:

a. The importance of customer care and relationship marketing and the role that telephone operatives in your Call Centre play in this process.

(10 marks)

b. The key stages which would be involved in developing a Customer Care Programme for your Call Centre.

(10 marks)
(20 marks in total)

Question 6.

You work as a Promotions Assistant for an industrial company of your choice, and it is your job to outline the company's promotions plans for the coming year. Draft an informal report to your Promotions Manager indicating which promotions tools you believe would be most effective, and explain why.

(20 marks)

Question 7.

You have been appointed to the position of Communications Manager for a large airline company.

a. Using illustrations from the airline business, draft notes for a presentation to staff explaining the benefits of using visual methods to convey complex data.

(10 marks)

b. Draft notes for a presentation to your marketing team, explaining how implementing the latest Information and Communications Technology (ICT) tolls can help improve communications and relationships with customers.

(10 marks)
(20 marks in total)

Appendix 4

Feedback to the specimen examination paper

The following do not represent full specimen answers to the Specimen Examination Paper, but look at:

- The rationale for the question – what the examiner is looking for.
- The best way to structure your answer.
- The key points that you should have included, and expanded upon.
- How marks for the question might have been allocated.
- The main syllabus area that is being assessed.

Note that many of the key points are represented here in the form of bullet point lists. All of these points should be expanded in your answer, unless the examiner **specifically** asks for a bullet point list.

The timings given for each part of each question allow a little time for reading the Case Study, planning your answers, and choosing which questions you will answer. Remember to follow the instructions on the paper.

The following feedback provides guidelines on how to structure your answers and what to include, with hints about which Sessions will help you. In some cases you may have presented the information in a different way that would be acceptable.

Part A

The Case Study provides data and information from the UK Small Car Market.

Question 1.

1a.

The task is to use the information provided to make recommendations for how the Fiesta should be marketed in the future. The examiner has asked for report format so set your answer out as follows:

REPORT

Report to: A. Biggs, Marketing Manager
Prepared by: C. Dodds, Product Manager
Date: 14 November 200X

1. Terms of Reference

The aim of this report is to make recommendations for the future marketing of the Ford Fiesta following discussion of key trends in the UK Small Car Market identified from analysis of printed articles in the consumer and trade press.

The report has been commissioned by the Marketing Manager.

2. Methodology

Information on the UK Small Car Market has been researched from using articles printed in Car Market based on research conducted in 1998 by Lifestyle Research.

3. Findings

Set out the findings under sub-headings such as:

3.1 Manufacturers' spend on advertising.
3.2 Recall of advertising.
3.3 Consumer buyer behaviour.
3.4 Performance of Fiesta in UK Small Car Market.

4. Conclusions

5. Recommendations

1b.

(See formats shown in Session 3).

i) Draw a line graph with the title of 'Recall of Advertising in Past Month' (% Drivers) with Car Manufacturers on the horizontal X axis and % Drivers on the vertical Y axis. Accredit source of information.

ii) A component bar chart is also known as a stacked bar chart. Put the different home types on the X axis and % owned on the vertical axis. Add legend, heading and accreditation.

iii) On the pie chart label each sector with the model of car, number sold expressed as a figure and a percentage. Add title and accreditation.

Area of the syllabus covered: 4.5, 4.8.

Part B

Question 2.

2a.

The agenda should be written on headed note paper. (See the notes in Session 4).

XYZ Company

Meeting to discuss advertising campaign for Product X

Date: 12 October 200X
Time: 2pm-4pm
Meeting Room 6

Agenda

1.	Apologies for absence	Chair
2.	Minutes of previous meeting	Chair
3.	Matters arising	Chair
4.	Sales results from previous quarter	Sales Manager
5.	Presentation on new advertising campaign	Product Manager
6.	Discussion on promotional support	All
7.	AOB	Chair
8.	Date of next meeting	Chair

2b.

Use a memo format as set out in Session 3 and include the following:

Planning using PASS.
Advice on delivery (including how to overcome nerves as the Product Manager has very little experience), design of visual aids, maintaining audience interest and handling the question and answer session at the end.

Area of the syllabus covered: 4.1-4.7.

Question 3.

The question tells you what information to include in the letter. However, when constructing the letter remember what the sponsor will be looking for – information that suggests that it is appropriate to align the company's name with the dog's home so make sure you emphasise the benefits for the sponsor. (Use a letter format as set out in Session 3).

Other information that should be included is the cost, the length of time the sponsorship deal is expected to cover and how their company will be acknowledged as sponsors – position of logo, information on the organisation etc.

Also enclose a copy of a previous newsletter for information.

Area of the syllabus covered: 1.2, 1.4, 2.2, 2.4, 3.2, 3.8, 4.8.

Question 4.

(Refer back to Session 9).

An opportunity to let your imagination and creativity come to the fore! The question provides you with some information about essential information to be included. Your advertisement might be set out similar to the one below:

Picture

Life is not all work and no play for ABC's Product Managers!

ABC Toys are seeking an energetic and creative Product Manager to:
(give some information about the job and the reward).

ABC Toys is the leading toymaker of (provide company information).

For application form and further details please contact: (add contact details).

LOGO

Give printing and layout instructions to the production department for the main headline, logo position and paragraphs to include font type, size, special effects such as bold and alignment. For example:

1. Picture to be centred, full colour photograph (to be supplied from company archive Ref: JP1002) and sized to cover 25% of page.

2. Headline, "Life is not......... Product Managers" centred with Product Managers on the second line as shown, bold, font size 22.

3. ....

Advertisement to be printed in Marketing Recruitment, inside left page on 3rd and 10th January 200X.

Area of the syllabus covered: 3.2-3.7.

Question 5.

Email format is similar to memo format. Identify receiver, sender and subject. Emails are dated.

As with previous questions use the situation that you are given in the question to put your answer into context.

At the beginning of your email identify who you are, why you were asked to carry out the research and your findings.

Then provide the information on the importance of customer care and relationship marketing (see Sessions 2 and 5) with particular emphasis on the role of the telephone operatives – how they contribute to this. As email is a less formal communication than report you may wish to use bullet points.

The telephone operatives are front-line staff so concentrate on the importance of good telephone technique when they are communicating with customers plus their role in gathering information about customer likes and dislikes.

A customer care programme provides a structured approach that can be managed. Training will be required before it is fully operational. Identify the key stages in setting it up – gathering information, setting standards, identifying controls, management, dealing with failures (complaints) and carrying out training to implement programme. Identify the benefits of a programme in developing the culture of customer care. Consider any constraints afforded by the call centre environment.

Area of the syllabus covered: 1.2-1.4, 4.8, 5.1-5.5.

Question 6.

This is an informal report so it should be presented under headings but does not require the formality of the report completed earlier. It can be set out similarly to a memo but the information must be structured and presented under headings.

Report to: **C. Chubb, Promotions Manager**
From: **F. Fisher, Promotions Assistant**
Subject: **Promotion Plans for Product X**
Date of Report: **26 May 200X**

Purpose of Report

The purpose of this report is to ....

Select an industrial company that you have some knowledge of and identify the range of products that is being promoted and the target audience.

As this is an informal report you may write in the first person.

Outline the promotional mix under separate headings for advertising, sales promotion etc. (Refer back to Sessions 7-11).

Justify your decisions and identify why the mix you suggest is effective.

Note any assumptions you make.

At the close identify what action you will take next.

Area of the syllabus covered: 1.2, 2.1-2.5, 3.1-3.13, 4.8.

Question 7.

7a.

The first part of this question is about producing notes for a presentation on the benefits of using visual methods such as graphs and charts to present complex data. It is not a question about the airline industry. However, use examples from the airline industry to illustrate your points, such as using visual methods to convey complex information for staff, project teams and annual report. Use your imagination but remember who you are (Communications Manager) and who the audience is (staff of the airline industry). A structure for presenting the answer is given below with guidelines for what you should include. (Refer back to Sessions 3 and 4).

Use PASS to plan the presentation (adding your assumptions):

Purpose – as above.
Audience – staff of the airline industry – what do they need to know?
Venue, dates and time.
Structure – what are the main points?
Style – how are you going to present?

Introduction – introduce self and presentation.

Main body – cover points such as:

- Why use visual methods to convey information.
- Types of information that are best presented visually (remember to use examples from airline industry).
- Guidelines for presenting graphs and charts such as line graph, pie chart, bar graph, tables and diagrams.

Summary

Repeat main points, take questions and thank staff for attending.

7b.

The second part of the question asks for draft notes for a presentation so bullet point the main points you want to use about the use of ICT to improve **communications and relationships** with customers. Remember to use the context of the airline company you work for. (Refer to Sessions 2, 5 and 12).

Think of as many examples as you can but put them in context – some are included below.

This part of the question is about the benefits for customers so consider main contact points such as their need to gather information (digital and interactive TV, web site), promoting special deals (direct mail, WAP), booking (online for example), dealing with enquiries (automated call handling) arriving for the flight, in flight and arriving at their destination. Do not forget dealing with complaints. How can ICT improve the ability of the organisation and staff to communicate and develop effective relationships with customers at all points?

Also include the way ICT improves the ability of staff to communicate internally (videoconferencing for international contacts) with each other and suppliers (ISDN lines for data exchange, Extranet). How are relationships enhanced by the use of technology?

The main structure of your answer can be:

Introduction – self and presentation.
Main body – bulleted main points as above.
Summary – close, take questions and thank audience.

Area of the syllabus covered: 3.14, 4.3, 4.7, 5.4, 5.6.

Appendix 5

Assessment guidance

There are two methods used for assessment of candidates – Examination <u>or</u> Continuous Assessment via projects.

The Chartered Institute of Marketing has traditionally used professional, externally set examinations as the means of assessment for the Certificate, Advanced Certificate and Postgraduate Diploma in Marketing. In 1995, at the request of industry, students and tutors, it introduced a continuously assessed route to two modules, one at Certificate level, and one at Advanced Certificate. With an increased emphasis on marketing practice, all modules are now open to assessment through examination or assessed project.

The information in this Appendix will:

- Help you prepare for continuous assessment.
- Provide hints and tips to help you prepare for the examination.
- Manage your time effectively in preparing for assessment.

NB: Your tutor will inform you which method of assessment applies to your programme.

Preparing for continuous assessment

If you are being assessed by project you will be given a full brief for the assignment. This will include what you have to do, how it is to be presented, and the weighting of marks for each section. **YOU MUST READ THIS BEFORE YOU START, AND CHECK YOUR UNDERSTANDING OF WHAT IS BEING ASKED OF YOU WITH YOUR TUTOR.**

The assignment will consist of a number of tasks, each with their own weighting, so make sure you take account of this in your final presentation of the project.

The size of the project will be identified by a recommended word count. Check your final word count carefully, but remember quality is more important than quantity.

The assignment tasks will include a reflective statement. This requires you to identify what you have learned from the experience of undertaking the module, and how you have applied that learning to your job.

Questions you might want to consider in helping you write this reflective statement include: What was the most difficult part? How did you feel at the start of the exercise and how do you feel at the end? Did you achieve your objectives? If not, why not? What have you learned about yourself as you have worked through the module? How much of your learning have you been able to apply at work? Have you been able to solve any real work problems through the work you have done in your assignments?

This statement will be personal to you, and it should look forward to the points you have identified as needing work in the future. The effective marketer never stops learning. You should keep up this process of Continuous Professional Development as you go through your studies and your career, and hopefully you will have acquired the habit by the time you need to employ it to achieve Chartered Marketer status!

Examinations

Each subject differs slightly from the others, and the style of question will differ between module examinations. All are closed book examinations apart from **Analysis and Decision** (see below).

For all examinations, apart from **Marketing in Practice** (see below), the examination paper consists of two sections:

Part A – Mini case, scenario or article

This section has a mini case, scenario or article with compulsory questions. You are required to make marketing or sales decisions based on the information provided. You will gain credit for the decisions and recommendations you make on the basis of the analysis itself. This is a compulsory section of the paper designed to evaluate your practical marketing skills.

Part B – Examination questions

You will have a choice from a number of questions, and when answering those you select, ensure you understand the context of the question. Rough plans for each answer are strongly recommended.

The examination for **Marketing in Practice** differs in that the compulsory questions and examination questions are all linked to the mini case and additional relevant information given, such as memos and reports.

The examination for **Analysis and Decision** is an open book examination and takes the form of a Case Study. This is mailed out 4 weeks before the examination and posted on the CIM student web site (www.cimvirtualinstitute.com) at the same time. Analysis and preparation should be completed during these four weeks. The questions asked in the examination will require strategic marketing decisions and actions. The question paper will also include additional unseen information about the Case Study.

CIM code of conduct for examinations

If being assessed by examination you will receive examination entry details, which will include a leaflet entitled "Rules for Examinations". You should read these carefully, as you will be penalised by CIM if you are in breach of any of these rules.

Most of the rules are common sense. For example, for closed book examinations you are not allowed to take notes or scrap paper into the examination room, and you must use the examination paper supplied to make rough notes and plans for your answer.

If you are taking the **Analysis and Decision** examination ensure that you do take your notes in with you, together with a copy of the Case Study.

Hints and tips

There are a number of places you can access information to help you prepare for your examination, if you are being assessed by this method. Your tutor will give you good advice, and exam hints and tips can also be found on the CIM student web site (www.cimvirtualinstitute.com).

Some fundamental points are listed below.

- Read the question carefully, and think about what is being asked before tackling the answer. The examiners are looking for knowledge, application and context. Refer back to the question to help you put your answer in the appropriate context. Do not just regurgitate theory.
- Consider the presentation style of your answer. For example, if you are asked to write a report, then use a report format with number headings and not an essay style.
- Structure – plan your answer to make it easy for the examiner to see the main points you are making.

- Timing – spread your time in proportion to the marks allocated, and ensure that all required questions are answered.
- Relevant examples – the examiners expect relevant theory to be illustrated by practical examples. These can be drawn from your own experience, reading of current journals and newspapers, or just your own observations. You could also visit "Hot Topics" on the CIM student web site to see discussions of topical marketing issues and practice.

Managing your time

What is effective time management? It is using wisely one of your most precious resources, **TIME,** to achieve your key goals. You need to be aware of how you spend your time each day. Set priorities, so you know what's important to you and what isn't. You need to establish goals for your study, work and family life, and plan how to meet those goals. Through developing these habits you will be better able to achieve the things that are important to you.

When study becomes one of your key goals you may find that, temporarily, something has to be sacrificed to find the time needed for reading, writing notes, writing up assignments, preparing for group assessment, etc. It helps to "get people on your side". Tell people that you are studying and ask for their support – this includes direct family, close friends and colleagues at work.

Time can just slip through your fingers if you don't manage it, and that's wasteful! When you are trying to balance the needs of family, social life, working life and study, there is a temptation to leave assignments until the deadline is nearly upon you. Don't give in to this temptation! Many students complain about the heavy workload towards the end of the course, when, in fact, they have had several months to work on assignments, and they have created this heavy workload themselves.

Knowing how to manage your time wisely can help you:

- Reduce pressure when you're faced with deadlines or a heavy schedule.
- Be more in control of your life by making better decisions about how to use your time.
- Feel better about yourself because you're using your full potential to achieve.

- Have more energy for the things you want or need to accomplish.
- Succeed more easily because you know what you want to do and what you need to do to achieve it.

Finally…

Remember to continue to apply your new skills within your job. Study and learning that is not applied just wastes your time, effort and money! Good luck with your studies!

Index

See also the Glossary on page 234.

You may find referring back to the Learning Outcomes and the Summary of Key Points at the beginning and end of each Session will aid effective use of the Index.

Only where subjects are relevantly discussed or defined are they indexed.